DICTIONARY OF
CALORIES

DICTIONARY OF
CALORIES

Bloomsbury Books
London

This edition published 1994 by Bloomsbury Books, an imprint of The Godfrey Cave Group, 42 Bloomsbury Street, London, WC1B 3QJ.

ISBN 1 85471 510 0

Printed and bound in France by Maury Eurolivres

Contents

Introduction

Why are people overweight? The simple answer is that they overeat. This means that more energy (calories) is taken in through food than is expended in energy (activity). This simple truth can be expressed in the form of the 'Energy Equation'.

Calories *in, more than* Energy *out* = Weight *gain*

The excess calories are stored as body fat and excess weight is the result.

Whatever you might think, having 'big bones' or a 'heavy frame' do not necessarily make you fat.

In practical terms, you must alter the energy equation so that your calorie input is less than your activity output. You can do this simply by reducing the amount you eat.

For *safe and healthy* weight loss, do not reduce your total daily calories below 1000, unless you are under medical supervision. When you drastically cut your food intake, you body perceives a state of starvation and adjusts the metabolic rate to cope on the reduced amount of 'fuel'. This means that you will not lose weight. If you then increase your food intake, your body's lowered metabolic rate does not burn it up so effectively, so you will gain even more weight.

Don't get caught in this irritating 'Catch 22'. Reduce calorie intake gradually, and you will achieve a steady and more lasting reduction in weight.

For *most effective* weight loss, increase your daily activity as well as reducing your calories (see 'Exercise').

Slimming seems simple, yet many slimmers fail because our relationship with food is a complex one. Successful slimming is based upon knowledge of the following:

- psychological factors that affect efforts to diet
- appropriate action

Things you should know about

...Weighing yourself

This does not have to be a depressing or self-deceiving exercise if you keep to a few rules.

Use the same scales.

Keep the scales in *exactly* the same place, or they may weigh differently.

Weigh at the same time of the day, preferably first thing in the morning.

Wear a similar weight of clothes, preferably none.

Weigh yourself only once a week. Weight loss is a relatively slow process, so don't court disappointment by weighing yourself more often. Too-frequent weighing may also encourage obsession.

Stand still on the scales, distributing your weight evenly.

Advertisements — and other people — sometimes boast of weight losses that are both huge and fast, and may create unrealistic expectations in you.

Try not to be impatient. Weight lost rapidly may be unhealthy, and may be regained equally rapidly.

As a rough guide, a safe and healthy weight loss for most people is an *average* of 2 lb/1 kg per week. Note that weight-loss may vary from week to week.

...Weight loss and contraception

Women using the diaphragm method of birth control should note that a weight loss of more than 7 lb/3 kg could mean that their contraceptive device no longer fits properly, and that pregnancy might result. Remember to consult your family planning adviser as soon as necessary.

...PMS and slimming

Woman who suffer from PMS (Pre-menstrual Syndrome), sometimes find that, for a few days before a period, temporary fluid retention causes additional weight, and may mask an actual fat-loss.

Other symptoms of PMS, such as depression, tension, or a craving for carbohydrates, may also adversely affect dieting behaviour. Keep notes of your symptoms and consult your doctor and/or one of the national associations concerned with PMS (see 'Useful Addresses' and 'Further Reading').

...Change of Life

Menopausal symptoms may cause problems that also interfere with your slimming efforts. Do not feel that you are doomed to suffer unaided. You could consult your doctor, a well-woman clinic, and/or the books suggested (see 'Useful Addresses' and 'Further Reading'). If you doctor proves unsympathetic, remember that you are entitled to change your GP if you wish.

...Eating with the family.

Slimmers can easily eat with the family if they follow the guidelines in 'Cook Slim'. Delicious meals can be created, which will have health benefits for the whole family. Families can be very resistant to change, so make changes to the family meals without drawing attention to them.

...Entertaining

Apply the 'Cook Slim' guidelines here too. Your dinner guests will never suspect — they will merely be delighted with the results!

Look out for cookery books containing low-fat recipes (see 'Useful Reading') and amend your favourite recipes as the 'Cook Slim' guidelines suggest.

Your Ideal Weight

It is important to remember that height/weight charts supply only a general guide to suitable weights. They are often based upon statistics from life insurance companies and show desirable, 'healthy' weights in relation to height. However, individuals vary greatly, and what might be ideal for one person's frame, may not be so for another. Consequently, most height/weight charts provide a range of acceptable weights relative to each height.

...Using the chart

Do get some help to check your height — don't guess.

Do not set yourself an ideal weight so far below your existing weight that it intimidates you immediately. It is not always necessary to set a target at the outset. You could simply allow yourself to lose some weight, and thus gain confidence first.

Do use common sense in assessing your shape and the amount of obvious body fat. However, it is not always easy to see yourself objectively, so also ask the opinion of someone you trust, and/or your doctor.

Do remember that it is natural for women to have more body-fat than men.

Do not become obsessed about your weight or shape. You *do not* have to match some fashion magazine ideal.

Men's Medical Weight Chart

Height		Average Weight		Obese	
m	(ft in)	stone lb	(kg)	stone lb	(kg)
1.55	(5,1)	8,12	(56)	10, 8	(67)
1.58	(5,2)	9,1	(58)	10,13	(69)
1.60	(5,3)	9,4	(59)	11,2	(71)
1.63	(5,4)	9,7	(60)	11,5	(72)
1.65	(5,5)	9,11	(62)	11,11	(75)
1.68	(5,6)	10,1	(64)	12,1	(77)
1.70	(5,7)	10,5	(66)	12,7	(79)
1.73	(5,8)	10, 9	(68)	12,11	(81)
1.75	(5,9)	10,13	(69)	13,1	(83)
1.78	(5,10)	11,4	(72)	13,8	(86)
1.80	(5,11)	11,8	(74)	13 12	(88)
1.83	(6,0)	11,13	(76)	14,5	(91)
1.85	(6,1)	12,3	(78)	14,9	(93)
1.88	(6,2)	12,8	(80)	15,2	(96)
1.91	(6,3)	12,13	(82)	15,7	(98)

Women's Medical Weight Chart

Height		Average Weight		Obese	
m	(ft in)	stone lb	(kg)	stone lb	(kg)
1.42	(4,8)	7,4	(46)	8,10	(55)
1.45	(4,9)	7,6	(47)	8,12	(56)
1.47	(4,10)	7,9	(49)	9,3	(59)
1.50	(4,11)	7,12	(50)	9,6	(60)
1.52	(5,0)	8,1	(51)	9,9	(61)
1.55	(5,1)	8,4	(53)	10,0	(64)
1.58	(5,2)	8,8	(54)	10,4	(65)
1.60	(5,3)	8,11	(56)	10,7	(67)
1.63	(5,4)	9,2	(58)	11,0	(70)
1.65	(5,5)	9,6	(60)	11,4	(72)
1.68	(5,6)	9,10	(62)	11,10	(74)
1.70	(5,7)	10,0	(64)	12, 0	(76)
1.73	(5,8)	10,4	(65)	12,4	(78)
1.75	(5,9)	10,8	(67)	12,10	(81)
1.78	(5,10)	10,12	(69)	13,0	(83)

Slimming—Why bother?

There's no doubt about it — slimming is a demanding, sometimes difficult task, but the benefits are rewarding, and sometimes even elating. What will slimming do for you?

It's only natural... Slimness can be seen as the 'natural' state for human beings. Our early ancestors scavenged, hunted and fished for food — an active lifestyle that helped them slim. It was only later that 'civilisation' ruined their eating habits — and their figures — with over-refined, over-sugary and over-advertised foods.

It's easier... to romp with the children, to enjoy physical games and exercise, to make love, to run for a bus, to walk the dog... and get into a sports car!

It's healthier... Excess weight is associated with high blood pressure, heart disease, stroke, kidney ailments, gallstones, diabetes, varicose veins, gynaecological problems and difficulties with physical coordination.

It's more attractive... despite what the 'Fat Liberation Movement' says. It is unhelpful, and even irresponsible, to preach that 'big is beautiful' when the health hazards are so great. Slimming is not simply a vanity — it also shows respect for our bodies and ourselves.

It's worth it... As one successful slimmer said, 'I didn't know how unfit I was. Until I lost weight, I just didn't know what I was missing!'

Why should *you* miss out?

... Start slimming now!

Chubby Children

Being fat isn't fun — particularly for children. Playground taunts can be very cruel, and such treatment can sew the seeds of behaviour in later life — perhaps resulting in an unhappy relationship with food which might lead to anorexia or bulimia (see 'Eating Disorders').

It's no good making excuses: 'Heaviness runs in the family. We're all on the large size.' It is both unfair and unkind to inflict fatness and your poor eating habits on your children.

Start young with good eating habits, and ignore the old adage that a fat baby is a healthy baby — it's not usually true. Serve your children nutritious food that is low in fat, sugar and salt, and high in fibre. If they never develop a taste for sugary treats and highly processed foods, they're unlikely to do so in adulthood.

It is a common habit to give food as a reward or for comfort. While this may stop tears or keep children quiet, it is not a good idea on a regular basis. In most instances, a cuddle, a chat or a few minutes of your time to play a game would be just as effective — and calorie-free!

If your children are already overweight, start a healthier approach to food right now. Apply all the principles discussed in 'Eat Slim', 'Cook Slim' and overleaf, and they need never feel deprived or hungry. Whilst it is advisable to keep your children to a healthy eating regime, if your child is overweight you should seek medical advice before putting a diet plan in hand.

Some tips for happy and healthy family meals

• Avoid giving babies food with added sugar. Puddings and rusks frequently contain very high amounts of sugar, so don't serve them. Real labels carefully.

• Give fresh fruit rather than sweets as a snack or treat. There are lots of exotic varieties to choose from, such as mango, kiwi, tangello and kumquats.

• Make sure your children have a good breakfast and they'll be less likely to snack.

• Always use wholemeal bread — it's more nutritious and more filling.

• Serve favourite foods, such as beefburgers, fish fingers and chips only occasionally, choosing the best quality, low-fat varieties available. Grill or oven-bake, rather than fry these foods.

• Make your own beefburgers using low-fat mince.

• Buy low-sugar baked beans and ketchup.

• Serve baked potatoes rather than chips.

• Cut down gradually on puddings and offer fresh fruit, instead.

Eating Disorders

In any text about slimming, it is important to mention the hazards of taking it too far. Loss of appetite and excessive eating are sometimes symptoms of specific illnesses. For example, it is normal to be 'off your food' if you have 'flu'. However, if eating patterns are distorted in otherwise healthy people, they are said to be suffering from eating disorders.

The most well known of these disorders are anorexia and bulimia nervosa. Both are usually found in less assertive individuals whose repressed feelings may be expressed through their relationship with food.

Around 90 per cent of sufferers are female, but the incidence of male sufferers is constantly increasing.

...What is anorexia?

The word 'anorexia' means 'loss of appetite', but the disorder is much more complex than that. It is sometimes referred to as 'slimmer's disease', but this term is misleading, for anorexics are more concerned with achieving autonomy than slimness. They often feel helpless and inadequate, even though appearing confident.

Anorexics progressively reduce food intake in a pursuit of thinness that is valued as proof of control, rather than as a sign of beauty. It is accompanied by a delusion about true body size and a fear that if normal eating recommences, they will be unable to stop.

It is rare for sufferers to seek help, as they do not usually recognise the syndrome and its dangers. However, they need expert help as soon as possible and should be persuaded to consult a doctor or self-help agency as a matter of urgency (see also 'Further Reading' and 'Useful Addresses').

...What is bulimia?

The word 'bulimia' means 'great hunger', but the syndrome is much more complex than that. Massive urges to overeat and built up, which are satisfied by binge-eating. This is followed by efforts to rid the body of the food's potential fattening effects by purging with laxatives or diuretics, by self-induced vomiting, or by crash/starvation dieting.

There are links between anorexia and bulimia, and some bulimics (albeit a minority) have previously been anorexics. Consequently, the disorder is also referred to as 'bulimarexia'. The nature of this disorder means that, while eating huge amounts of food, some bulimics remain slim others undergo wild fluctuations in weight, gaining and losing as much as 100 lb/45 kg between phases of bingeing and purging.

Bulimia is often a secret syndrome accompanied by feelings of shame and disgust. Food is viewed less with pleasure, than with fear.

Social pressures to be slim seem to be a major factor in causing bulimia. The fashion for thinness is aided and abetted by an opportunist 'diet industry' promoting the idea that 'thin is beautiful', while advertisers simultaneously extol the delights of fattening foods, and social habits encourage eating almost as a pastime.

The tension and anxiety that these contradictory messages cause may result in people opting for crash or starvation diets in an attempt to get quick results. Such dieting deprives the body of the nutrients it needs and triggers off food cravings. When the tension and/or body's cravings are resolved by binge-eating, bulimia is but a short step away. Initially, slimmers may see the purging that inevitably follows bingeing as a good way of controlling weight gain, but they are often unaware of the disastrous consequences. Through constant purging, but they are often unaware of the disastrous consequences.

Bulimia has serious physical and emotional effects on the body. These include dizziness, headaches, fatigue, abdominal cramps, gum disease, severe constipation, erratic or stopped periods, irritability and depression. Bulimics *must* seek specialist help, either through their GP or a sufferer's support group (see 'Further Reading' and 'Useful Addresses'). Make sure that you don't replace your weight problem with another that is potentially more lethal.

Quiz 1
What kind of thinker are you?

Read the questions and choose (honestly) the answer (A,B, or C) that applies to you.

1 You think you have had a 'good week' of dieting. You get on the scales, but you have lost *no* weight. Do you:

> A Feel furious and decide it's time to abandon slimming?
>
> B Feel annoyed and promise yourself a treat (food) to console yourself?
>
> C Think critically about everything you *did* eat to see if you could have done better?

2 You have a 'good day' dieting. Then someone offers you a cake, which you eat. Do you:

> A Think, 'Oh well, I've blown it. I might as well have another piece'?
>
> B Think, 'That little bit won't hurt'?
>
> C Make up for it by cutting down later — and tomorrow?

3 You see your favourite cream cakes in the baker's window. Do you think:

    A 'I want one now' — and have one?

    B 'I want one now' — but don't have one?

    C This doesn't apply to you — you avoid cake shops.

4 You read a 'Before and After' story. Do you think:

    A 'How marvellous! But I couldn't get as slim as that'.

    B 'I think they fake these pictures'.

    C 'If she can do it, so can I'.

5 You see a slim, attractive woman whose shape you admire. Do you think:

    A 'I bet she can eat anything she likes, yet stay slim'.

    B 'I wish I was lucky like her'.

    C 'I bet she has to work at keeping a shape like that'.

Analysis and Tips

Mostly A answers

These answers indicate 'negative' thinking, characterised by 'I can't', 'I wish' and lack of hope. Negative thought is very destructive to a slimmer's motivation. Worse, it becomes a bad habit, dooming a diet to failure.

You need to:

Change how you think.

Monitor your thoughts. If they are negative, stop and rephrase them to optimistic ones.

Re-read the C answers in the quiz (the positive ones), and replace your negative thoughts with those.

Change 'I can't' into 'I can' in your thoughts — and you will!

Mostly B answers

These answers indicate 'rationalisation' thoughts. That is, making excuses for behaviour you really know is unhelpful.

You need to:

Recognise that inappropriate eating is always your own responsibility and your own choice.

Remind yourself that excuses can't get you slim — or excuse you.

Find ways other than overeating to reward yourself.

Mostly C answers

These answers indicate 'positive thinking' — the optimism that augurs well for success in slimming.

You need to:

Read both analysis and tips above.

Expand your positive thinking.

Re-read the C (positive) answers in the quiz and use them.

Remember: Improve your thinking and you'll improve your slimming.

Quiz 2
What kind of eater are you?

Answer each question (honestly) with 'yes', 'sometimes' or 'no'. Read the analysis and tips.

Section 1: Do you:

    A Have a snack, a taste, or nibble, when preparing meals?

    B Finish all the food on your plate?

    C Have a snack or nibble while watching TV

    D Eat more than you should in restaurants, or when eating in other people's houses?

    E Find the smell of good food irresistable?

    F Eat while standing up, or in the car, or in rooms of the house other than your dining area?

Section 2: Do you:

    A Eat because you feel unhappy or depressed?

    B Eat when you're bored?

    C Occasionally get a sudden, uncontrollable urge to eat?

    D Eat food that you don't really like if the urge to eat is strong?

E Eat more than usual if you are worried, anxious or under stress?

F Eat when not really hungry, if tempting food
is offered?

Analysis and Tips

Section 1: If you answered 'yes' or 'sometimes' to four or
more of these questions, your eating is strongly determined
by 'external cues'. This means that the sight and/or smell of
food act on you as 'triggers', influencing you to eat.

You need to:

Reorganise your life to avoid the sight and smell of food.

Keep all food at home out of sight; tempting treats should be
inaccessible — even taped up in containers, if necessary.

Alter walking routes to avoid tempting shops.

Avert your eyes in the supermarket from 'impulse buy' dis-
plays at the checkout.

Put less food on your plate, and use a smaller plate.

Obey the rule that you eat *only* when sitting in the dining area
at home or work.

Never eat while engaged in another activity.

Display prominently a note: 'Eat for need not greed'.

Section 2: If you answered 'yes' or 'sometimes' to four or
more of these questions, your eating is strongly determined
by your emotions. You may be abusing food as a tranquilliser

or anti-depressant — eating to solve problems. This fails. It merely gives you another problem — that of excess weight.

You need to:

Decide what the problems are and take action to solve them. Some problems which prompt overeating are stress, marital disharmony, sexual problems, depression, anxiety boredom and anger (maybe repressed). Women may also have physical problems connected with periods, contraception, or the menopause. If you suspect that these, or any other problems, are at the root of your overeating, do not despair; self-help is often possible. See 'Further Reading' and 'Useful Addresses' for starting points.

Try classes in relaxation, yoga and/or exercise.

Keep repeating to yourself: 'Eating doesn't solve problems, it only makes me fat.'

Seek medical help if your weight is making you anxious.

Find other ways of rewarding yourself.

Other scores If you have 'yes' answers in both sections, you need to tackle both angles, as suggested. All 'no' answers? Were you being honest?

Health and Nutrition

In recent years it has been realised that good health, as well as a slim figure, is not so much a matter of luck as a matter of what we choose to eat.

Food is the 'fuel' that keeps the body in good working order and supplies the energy for all activities. It is composed of many different nutrients, each of which performs a different function in the body. As very few foods contain *all* the nutrients necessary for good health, it is important to eat a variety of foods to ensure a balanced diet.

There are five categories of food essential to health and vitality:

1 Protein:

This is used for building, maintenance and repair of body tissues. In children and teenagers it is also used for growth. Protein should be eaten every day and constitute 10-15 per cent of your daily calorie intake (2 oz/50 g for women, and 3-3/5 oz/75-90 g for men, depending on how active the lifestyle). There is little point in eating more protein than you require, as it is simply expelled in the urine or stored as fat. Good, low-fat sources of protein include poultry, white fish, eggs, soya products, cottage cheese and yoghurt. Other, less-rich sources include cereals, bread, rice, potatoes and pulses.

2 Carbohydrates

These are divided into three types: sugars, starches and fibre.

Sugar occurs naturally in certain foods, for example, fructose in fruit and lactose in milk. Refined sugar (sucrose), used in tea, coffee, biscuits and sweets, is an 'empty' food: it has no nutrients at all, so it is completely superfluous to dietary needs. Consuming sweet things raises the blood sugar level very quickly, but it drops again equally rapidly, so you still feel hungry and may even develop a craving for more sweet things. Sugar does you no good at all, so avoid it, or keep it to a minimum.

Starch is a tasteless white substance found in many foods, such as bread, potatoes, pasta, rice, cereals and beans. It tends to be bulky, so is useful for making the stomach feel full.

Fibre, sometimes call 'roughage', is an indigestible carbohydrate which cannot be absorbed by the body. It simply passes through the digestive tract, helping its efficiency, and reducing the risk of constipation and disease. Fibre is good news for slimmers as, when consumed with liquid, it helps to fill you up, so you eat less. (Note that high-fibre diets *must* be accompanied by lots of liquid — at least 3-4 pints/1.7-2.2 litres a day.) The recommended daily fibre intake for adults is about 1.25 oz/30 g. Good sources of fibre include bran cereals, sugar-free muesli, wholemeal products, jacket potatoes, lightly cooked vegetables, pulses and fruit (with skin when possible).

In their natural, unrefined state carbohydrates are an important source of energy and nutrition. They should account for 55-60 per cent of your daily calorie intake. Like any food, if you eat more than your body requires, the excess is stored as fat.

3 Fats and oils

These may be divided into three types: saturates, monounsaturates and polyunsaturates. All fats contain a mixture of the three, so they are labelled according to which type predominates.

Saturates, found in dairy products, meat (especially red), hard fats and coconut oil are not an essential part of the diet. In fact, they are believed to cause an accumulation of cholesterol in the blood which 'furs' the arteries and can lead to heart attacks. It is generally agreed that we should all avoid saturated fats and minimise consumption of high-cholesterol foods, such as egg yolks and liver.

Monounsaturates are present in olive oil, nuts and seeds, and should be consumed in preference to saturates.

Polyunsaturates are the only fats the body actually needs because they contain two essential fatty acids that cannot be synthesised by the body. However, the requirement is a mere 1.5 oz/4 g per day. Make sure the fats and oils you buy are labelled 'high in polyunsaturates'.

Given these facts, most people can afford to cut fat intake considerably. Weight for weight, fats have a higher calorific value than any other food, so they should be kept to a minimum in any slimming diet. Remember that some foods have a 'hidden' fat content: cakes, biscuits, pastries, ice-cream, chocolate and meat (even when visible fat has been removed). Try to avoid all these things and use low-fat substitutes whenever possible.

4 Vitamins

These enable the body to process foods so they can do their jobs properly. Fat-soluble vitamins (A, D, E and K) are stored in the liver and fatty tissues, but water-soluble vitamins (B group, C and folic acid) cannot be stored for long, so adequate amounts must be eaten every day.

Vitamin A

Found in carrots, liver, milk, butter, margarine, egg yolk, cheese, tomatoes, dark green vegetables, yellow and orange fruits, halibut and cod liver oils.

The B vitamins

1 (thiamin) — found in milk, lean bacon, pork, cod's roe, liver, kidney, pulses, peanuts, oatmeal, wholemeal flour and bread, white flour and bread, brewer's yeast, wheatgerm, enriched breakfast cereals.

B_2 (riboflavin) — found in milk, yoghurt, cheese, liver, kidney, egg, bran, brewer's yeast, curd cheese.

B_3 (niacin) — found in peanuts, peanut butter; wholemeal bread, brewer's yeast, meat, liver, coffee, beer, pulses, yeast extract, potatoes, enriched cereals.

B_6 (pyridoxine) — found in potatoes, leafy vegetables, whole grains and cereals, nuts, fresh and dried fruits.

B_{12} — found in liver, heart, sardines, cheese, eggs, milk.

Folic acid

Found in liver, fish, avocados, green vegetables, wholemeal bread, eggs, bananas, oranges, bran, beetroot, peanuts.

Vitamin C

Found in all fresh fruits and vegetables, but can be drastically reduced by prolonged cooking or storage. Good sources include blackcurrants, greens, raw cabbage, gooseberries, citrus fruits, guava, parsley, green and red peppers, mustard and cress, sprouts, watercress.

Vitamin D

Found in herrings, kippers, salmon, sardines, mackerel and pilchards, egg yolks, margarine, butter and liver. It is also produced by the action of sunlight on the skin.

Vitamin E

Found in dark green vegetables, wheat germ, vegetable oils, whole grains, nuts, eggs.

Vitamin K

Found in leafy vegetables, yoghurt, egg yolks.

5 Minerals

These do not mean a lot to most people, but they are vital to well-being. Among the essentials are:

Calcium, found in dairy products, sardines, soya beans, molasses, broccoli, peanuts and white bread. Women and girls should have up to 500 mg daily to lessen the risk of osteoporosis in later life.

Iodine, found in seafood, milk, eggs, meat, vegetables.

Iron, found in liver, kidney, beef, wholemeal bread, potatoes, watercress, dried apricots and soy sauce. Menstruating women and girls need a good supply of iron to lessen the chances of becoming anaemic.

Magnesium, found in vegetables and grains.

Phosphorus, found in nuts, eggs, soya and whole grains.

Potassium, found in milk, vegetables and fruit.

Sodium, found in most vegetables, often added as salt.

Zinc, found in milk, hard cheeses, wholemeal bread, meat, offal and shellfish, especially oysters.

Water is also essential to every bodily process. You should aim to drink around 3 pints/1.75 litre a day, whether straight from the tap or in the form of tea, coffee, or low-calorie drinks. Excess liquid is not stored as fat; it is simply expelled in the urine.

Eat Slim

Everyone is individual, so it follows that the amount of food each person needs will vary according to individual circumstances: constitution, age, sex and activity level. The chart below gives you an idea of the daily calorie intake to aim at for specific weight loss.

Approximate daily calorie intake

Amount to lose	*Women*	*Men (Sedentary/Active)*
Up to 14 lb/6 kg	1000	1500/2000
14-28 lb/6-12 kg	1250	1750-2000/2500-2750
Over 28 lb/12 kg	1500	2000-2500/2750-3000

Do not adhere rigidly to these guidelines. Experiment sensibly to see what intake suits you, and amend it accordingly. Remember to reduce your intake as the amount of weight to be lost decreases.

The following categories have special needs which must be taken into account when calculating calorie intake.

Tall people need more calories than shorter people.

Teenagers need about 20 per cent more, and should not have less than 1500 calories.

Children need more, relative to their body size. They should have not less than 1500, including a good supply of milk and yoghurt.

The elderly need 10-15 per cent less than the amount listed above. Reductions should be made particularly in foods high in fats and sugar.

Regardless of weight, we are all recommended to consume less fat, sugar and salt, and to eat more fibre. While it *is* possible to lose weight by consuming 1000 calories of chocolate per day, you would soon be suffering from malnutrition — and there is little point in losing weight at the expense of good health. Try some of the following tips to help you adjust your eating habits painlessly.

...To cut down portions

• Use a smaller plate.

• Eat more slowly, putting your knife and fork down between mouthfuls.

• Take smaller mouthfuls.

• Drink a glass of water or a cup of black tea or coffee, about ten minutes before you eat. This will take the edge off your appetite.

...To cut down on sugar

• Use artificial sweetener (not cyclamates) in hot drinks, and gradually reduce the amount you add.

• Choose low-calorie fizzy drinks rather than the regular variety.

• Add water to fruit juice (it contains a lot of natural sugar).

• Buy sugar-free or low-sugar foods, such as baked beans, canned fruit and muesli, wherever there is a choice.

• Try having fresh fruit instead of sweets or other sugary snacks.

...To cut down on salt

• Add salt at table rather than in cooking — you'll taste it more and thus use less.

• Try using low-sodium salt (half sodium, half potassium) to help you reduce your taste for it.

• Use other flavourings in food: garlic, lemon juice, herbs and spices.

• Avoid foods with high salt content, such as yeast extracts, crisps, peanuts and pickles.

...To cut down on fats/cholesterol

• Use low-fat dairy products for spreading, cooking and baking.

• Drink tea and coffee without milk.

• Use low-fat natural yoghurt instead of cream.

• Buy lean cuts of meat.

• Eat more fish.

• Grill rather than fry. If you must fry, use a non-stick pan, which requires less oil.

- Eat no more than four eggs (boiled or poached) per week.

...To increase fibre consumption

- Scrub rather than peel vegetables — the skins are good for you.
- Cook vegetables lightly.
- Eat lots of fresh fruit.
- Buy wholemeal bread, pasta and brown rice.
- Use wholemeal flour for cooking.
- Add beans and grains to soups and stews.

Planning your eating

Most people, including slimmers, eat three meals a day: breakfast, a light meal and a main meal. It does not matter whether you choose to eat your main meal at lunch or dinner. The important thing is to organise your eating to suit your lifestyle.

If you like to eat little but often, you can divide your daily food allowance into five smaller snack meals. Studies have suggested that more weight can be lost using this system than eating the same amount of food divided into three meals. Try it and see if it works for you.

However you choose to organise your eating, always keep the following points in mind.

• Eat at regular intervals. This benefits your body and avoids lengthy gaps between meals which may trigger snacking or a binge later.

• Weigh ingredients and portions. Estimating inevitably leads to overestimating, and thus overeating.

• Use leftovers as the basis of another meal, or throw them away. Do not finish them up yourself, even if you hate the thought of wasting good food.

• Do not eat later than nine o'clock. It's uncomfortable to go to bed with a full stomach and more importantly, your body cannot burn off the calories so efficiently.

Breakfast: A good way to start the day

Many slimmers eat no breakfast; it seems an easy meal to miss, and calories can be saved, but it is unwise to do so. The body has 'fasted' all night and its blood sugar levels are low. A balanced breakfast starts up the bodily system and helps us feel more awake and energetic, better able to cope with the morning. The slimmer who eats breakfast is less likely to turn to mid-morning snacks as a crutch or comfort. Those who miss breakfast will often find themselves craving something sweet, or even bingeing, later on. This craving is not due to poor will-power, but to a physiological need. It is the body's response to being deprived of the nutrients it needs. The awakening body is functioning at its lowest metabolic rate (i.e. the rate at which it burns up food into energy). The lower that rate remains the slower food is burned up, and therefore, the slower any weight loss. The very act of eating is believed to raise the metabolic rate (the 'thermogenic effect'), so breakfast can be good for those wanting to maximise weight loss.

...What's for breakfast?

As with any other meal, your choice of food is crucial. Bear in mind the information and tips given in the Health and Nutrition section and Eat Slim: aim to minimise fats and avoid refined sugar.

The six breakfast ideas below could easily be incorporated into a woman's diet of 1000 calories per day. Men in sedentary jobs may increase the amounts by half, while highly active men or manual workers may double them.

1

1 oz/25 g high-fibre cereal
$^1/_4$ pint/125 ml skimmed milk or low-fat yoghurt
or fruit (fresh or tinned, no added sugar)

2

1 slice bacon
1 grilled tomato
1 egg
1 oz/25 g bread

3

3 oz/75 g cottage cheese
2 slices crispbread or 2 oz/50 g bread or toast

4

2 oz/50 g toast
2 tomatoes and/or mushrooms

5

1 low-fat yoghurt
$^1/_2$ chopped apple
$^1/_2$ chopped banana

(substitute other fresh fruit, preferred)

6

2 oz/50 g wholemeal toast
$^1/_2$ oz/15 g low-fat spread

Tea or coffee, served black, with lemon or skimmed milk, would complete a nutritious but low-calorie start to the day.

Snacks

There should really be no need to snack if you're eating sensible meals, but in the first few days of a diet, you may experience hunger pangs while your stomach is adjusting to a lower food intake.

A glass of water or cup of tea will help to fill you up, but if you really must nibble, have a supply of celery and carrot sticks in the fridge, and keep the fruit bowl topped up.

Light Meals

What is a light meal? For some it could be an orange, for others it could be fish and chips. Keeping in mind your calorie allowance, a light meal should be satisfying enough to keep you from snacking between meals, and fulfil all the criteria outlined in the 'Health and Nutrition' section.

Below are some ideas for light meals that are nutritious and low in calories.

...Sandwiches

These are as good for you as what goes into them. Ideally, make them at home with wholemeal bread and low-fat spread or low-calorie mayonnaise. If you use a moist filling, you can omit the spread or mayonnaise completely and save a few calories.

To save time (and to avoid impulse over-eating if you are at home all day), make a batch of sandwiches, divide them into small packs and put them in the freezer, ready to eat as required.

Purchased sandwiches may exceed 450 calories per slice, so avoid them, if possible. If you do buy some, have them freshly made up with no butter, margarine or mayonnaise.

Low-calorie sandwich fillings

- 2 oz/50 g tuna (tinned in brine, not oil)
  mixed with a little chopped onion

- 1 oz/25 g mackerel (tinned in brine, not oil) mixed with a
  little low-calorie salad cream or mayonnaise

- 1 oz/25 g grated low-fat cheese with tomato
  and onion or sweet pickle or piccalilli

- 2 oz/50 g prawns mixed with low-calorie
  seafood dressing and lettuce

- 2 oz/50 g skinned, cooked chicken mixed with chopped
  onion and low-calorie salad cream or mayonnaise. If you
  like, add a little tandoori spice to the dressing.

Accompany your sandwiches with homemade coleslaw in low-calorie dressing. Finish your meal with one piece of fresh fruit of your choice.

...Jacket potatoes

The humble potato is a good source of nutrition and fibre and can make a hot and satisfying meal. Choose one weighing about 5 oz/150 g and try it with one of the fillings below.

Low-calorie potato fillings

- 3 oz/75 g cottage cheese

- 1 oz/25 g grated low-fat hard cheese with
  tomato and chopped onion

- 2 oz/ 50 g low-sugar baked beans

- 2 oz/50 g prawns with low-calorie mayonnaise

…Omelettes

Eggs are endlessly versatile and lend themselves to quick,
warming meals. For a low-calorie omelette, mix together two
eggs with a little skimmed milk and fry in a non-stick pan
without fat. Remember to limit your weekly egg consumption
to no more than two. For added flavour try the omelette with
one of the following.

- 1 oz/25 g chopped lean ham

- 2 chopped tomatoes

- 2 oz/50 g sliced mushrooms

- 1 tablespoon fresh chopped herbs, such as chives

…Soup

Homemade soups tend to be rather calorific, and may not always be to hand. For a light meal, use a packet of low-calorie
soup in the flavour of your choice. To make it more interesting, add some chopped vegetables (not potatoes) either raw or
cooked.

Main Meals

Your main meal of the day should be based on protein food, preferably fish or poultry. Red meats contain a lot of hidden fat, so choose lean pork rather than beef or lamb: it's less fattening.

To save time, you could prepare double quantities of such dishes as casseroles, chilli con carne and curry, keeping half to freeze for future use. Alternatively, keep a stock of purchased low-calorie meals. Although these can work out expensively, they are convenient and can be served with lightly-cooked fresh vegetables for a balanced meal.

Slimmers must abandon the traditional three-course main meal, except for special occasions or a weekend treat. Restrict the meal to one main course, and have fresh fruit or yoghurt instead of a pudding. On the occasions when a first course is needed, have low-calorie soup or melon.

Remember, food does not have to be hot to constitute a 'proper' meal. Cold lean meat and salad, for example, can be both satisfying and nutritious. Add a hot baked potato if you wish.

Read and put into practice the tips given in 'Eat Slim' and 'Cook Slim', then try some of the main meal ideas.

...Satisfying and slimming...

• Lean roast pork, lamb or beef with boiled potatoes and vegetables (3 oz/75 g meat per woman, and 4-5 oz/100-125 g per man)

• Skinless roast chicken or turkey with chosen vegetables (4 oz/100 g meat per woman, and 5-6 oz/125-150 g per man)

• Grilled pork or lamb chop with baked potato and chosen vegetables (the chop should weigh 5 oz/125 g per woman, and 6-7 oz/150-175 g per man)

• Lamb or pork chop casserole with onions and mushrooms, and sliced potato on top (quantities as above)

• Chicken or lamb's liver casserole with onions, mushrooms and tomatoes (quantities as roast pork)

• Cod in white, parsley or onion sauce made with skimmed milk (6 oz/ 150 g per woman, 7-8 oz/175-200 g per man)

• Hot or cold peppered mackerel with horseradish sauce, baked potato, peas, sweetcorn and/or coleslaw

• Wholemeal pasta dishes, such as lasagne or cannelloni, with a green salad

• Low-calorie prepared meals are 400 calories or less each. Serve with lightly-cooked vegetables.

• Stir-fry packs are quick and easy. Cook with water or two teaspoons of polyunsaturated oil. You can 'stretch' the pack for two people by adding chopped fresh vegetables, part cooked brown rice, and. if necessary, some cooked chopped meat

• French bread pizza, made by several frozen food manu- facturers, can be served with low-calorie coleslaw or fresh vegetables

Remember: boredom is a great enemy of the slimmer, so make your meals interesting and you'll be more successful in sticking to your diet.

'Safer' Shopping

It can be very daunting to the willpower to be confronted with so many temptations while shopping particularly in supermarkets. If you really want to avoid calorific buys, there are a few simple rules you can follow.

Avoid shopping when you feel hungry — you will be tempted to buy fattening snacks.

Take a shopping list with you — and stick to it.

Write out the shopping list while you are *not* hungry.

Take a low-calorie snack with you in case you are delayed. (A piece of crispbread, celery or carrot would suffice.)

Carry powdered skimmed milk in an empty tablet bottle to add to tea or coffee when out.

Take a flask of ready-made tea or coffee on outings to quieten hunger pangs and stave off impulse eating.

Avoid passing confectionery shelves or shops, if possible.

Discourage your children from eating sweets. This will protect *their* teeth from decay, and *you* from temptation.

Read food labels for calorie content and avoid products with added sugar. Even savoury products can contain sugar, so be selective. (See also 'Understanding Food Labels')

Don't buy 'economy' packs of chocolate or sugary treats; you know the economy turns to temptation once you get the pack home.

Inform the store manager if the diet foods you want , are not in stock.

Understanding Food Labels

By law, all food labels must show a complete list of the product's ingredients in descending order of weight. If, for example, sugar appears high in the list of ingredients, you know that the product contains quite a lot of it.

Unfortunately, additional laws making it compulsory to give other nutritional information are, as yet, only under consideration.

Don't be daunted by food labels — they're easy to understand once you have a little practice.

Nutrition

In addition to these ingredients, most labels list any additives the product contains. These frequently appear as E numbers. If you wish to find out more about additives, see 'Further Reading'.

Finally, beware products labelled 'suitable for diabetics' and vague claims, such as 'all natural'. Although diabetic foods contain no sugar, they have a high-calorie substitute, so they are not advantageous to slimmers. Similarly, claims about the 'natural' content of food does not preclude it having large amounts of sugar or saturated fat, both of which are naturally-occurring substances.

Slimmer's Shopping List

The slimmer's shopping list and store cupboard must be adapted to cater for new and healthier eating habits. Most of the items listed below are staples, so they are occasional rather than weekly buys. Substitute them for your usual items in each category. Remember: convenience foods are not necessarily junk foods. If in doubt, read the labels for sugar and fat content.

...Dairy produce

• skimmed milk

• low-fat spread, to replace butter and margarine. Note that margarines labelled 'high in polyunsaturates' are not low-calorie unless stated.

• low-fat, sugar-free yoghurt

• Smetana/low-fat sour cream, to replace ordinary cream

• low-fat hard cheeses

• low-fat soft cheeses

• low-fat cheese spreads

• low-fat processed cheese slices

...Breakfast cereals

- All-Bran
- Grape Nuts
- muesli mixture with no added sugar
- Nutrigrain

- fish, without batter or sauce
- seafood, such as prawns and mussels
- vegetables (freezing retains their vitamins and minerals)
- calorie-counted frozen meals
- skinless chicken pieces
- pre-packed mackerel, peppered or with mustard

Avoid processed and high-fat foods, such as beefburgers, sausages and meat pies, where the quality of the meat is uncertain and the proportion of fat to meat is usually high.

...Dry goods

- brown rice
- dried fruit
- wholemeal pasta
- pulses (beans, lentils, peas)
- wholemeal flour

...Tinned goods

- tuna and mackerel in brine, not oil
- salmon, especially Keta
- tomatoes
- low-sugar baked beans
- sugar-free corn kernels
- pulses (e.g. chick peas and kidney beans) need no soaking
- low-calorie soups
- fruit in natural juice or water not syrup

...Condiments

- low-calorie salad cream and mayonnaise
- oil-free salad dressing
- low-calorie vinaigrette
- low-calorie seafood dressing

...Spreads

- low-fat pâté (available in some supermarkets)
- low-sugar jams
- yeast extracts (use sparingly as they are high in salt)

...Herbs, spices and flavourings

Add extra interest to your cooking with some of the huge range of herbs, spices and flavourings currently available. You may well have a selection of the following items in stock already, so try some of the unusual ones, just for a change.

Herbs and spices: basil, bay leaves, cardamom, cayenne, pepper, chillies, chives, cinnamon, cloves, coriander, cumin, curry powder (preferably homemade), garlic/garlic granules, ginger, juniper, marjoram, nutmeg, oregano, paprika, parsley, rosemary, saffron, sage, tarragon, thyme, turmeric.

Flavourings: black peppercorns, linseeds, mustards, sesame seeds, soy sauce, *Tabasco* sauce, vinegars (wine, cider, fruit, herb, balsamic), Worcestershire sauce.

Try to minimise your use of salt and sugar If necessary use a low-sodium salt substitute and a low-calorie sweetener.

...Drinks

decaffeinated coffee (available in fresh and instant forms)

• low-calorie mixers, such as lemonade and ginger ale

• mineral waters (sparkling and still)

• fruit and herb teas

Avoid fruit juices, as they are high in natural sugars. Also avoid fruit 'drinks', which always contain added sugar.

Cook Slim

If you follow the advice in 'Eat Slim' and 'Safer Shopping', you're probably buying good food that is reasonably low in calories. However, it is essential to prepare it in a low-calorie way so that your sensible purchases don't turn into a dieting disaster.

Being the only slimmer in the household does not mean that you have to eat in isolation. In fact, the family need never know that you're trying to lose weight. They will all benefit from the low-fat, low-sugar, high-fibre approach to cooking, and your efforts can reap health dividends for everyone, decreasing excess weight where necessary, and giving protection against a variety of diet-related illnesses, especially heart disease.

...Food preparation

Cut off all visible fat from meat.

Remove all skin from poultry *before* cooking.

Weigh, do not guess your portions.

Scrub rather than peel vegetables.

Avoid nibbling.

...Useful equipment

Old habits need not die hard. Try using some of the items below in order to save nutritional content and minimise the use of fat in cooking.

Steamer — for fish and vegetables. This is clean and easy to use. although it is slower than boiling or baking. However, as the food is not sitting in water, valuable vitamins and minerals cannot leach out.

Wok — an ancient but highly efficient cooking implement that requires only a tiny amount of oil or water for cooking. Its shape helps to spread the heat quickly and evenly, so food can cook in minutes and thus retain its nutritional content.

Food processor — invaluable for chopping up vegetables, particularly for coleslaw.

Microwave cooker — great for baked potatoes, the hungry slimmer's healthy fast food.

...Cooking methods

• Dry fry in a non-stick pan whenever possible. If a recipe specifies pre-frying ingredients, simply miss out this step; you won't notice the difference in the finished dish. If you insist on frying, use two teaspoons of polyunsaturated oil, such as sunflower or rapeseed.

• Minced beef usually contains quite a lot of fat, so it may be dry-fried and the fat drained off before continuing with the recipe.

• Grill, poach, steam, bake, pressure-cook or microwave in preference to frying or roasting whenever possible.

• Avoid deep-frying. If you must cook chips, cut them straight and chunky, not thin or crinkly, so that they absorb less fat. All deep-fried foods should be a very occasional treat.

• Thicken casseroles by draining off the liquid and fast-boiling it to reduce. (Thickeners, such as cornflour or gravy granules, add lots of extra calories.)

• Avoid tasting dishes too often. Three or four spoonfuls of a sauce or gravy can contain a surprising number of calories. If you must taste, use a teaspoon.

...Healthy subsitutions

• Skimmed milk instead of whole milk in drinks, sauces, custard, milk puddings, mashed potatoes and scrambled eggs.

• Low-fat natural yoghurt for cream in casseroles and cake fillings. (Add it at the last minute to hot dishes to prevent it curdling.)

• Sorbet or yoghurt ice-cream instead of regular ice-cream or custard.

• Wholemeal pasta and brown rice for white varieties — they're more filling

• Wholemeal flour for white, or use half and half.

• Low-fat spread for butter and margarine.

• Jacket potatoes for chips and boiled potatoes.

• Low-fat roast potatoes for traditional ones (Cut larger, but fewer, chunks, brush lightly with oil and cook in a lightly-oiled roasting tin.)

Be open-minded about trying new dishes. Train yourself to unaccustomed flavours with small 'tasters' and experiment with different herbs and spices. There is no need to bore yourself with dull or repetitive food.

Try to adapt your favourite recipe, with the 'Cook Slim' guidelines in mind. If you're stuck for inspiration, borrow or buy some new cook books which specialise in low-fat, low-sugar cuisine (see 'Further Reading'). You'll soon discover that meals can be delicious as well as low-calorie and nutritious.

Entertaining

All the 'Cook Slim' tips should be applied when planning to entertain, whether for a small dinner party or a banquet for hundreds. With care and imagination, you can produce dishes that taste so good, your guests will never believe they're low-calorie and healthy.

Bear the following tips in mind to help the occasion go smoothly.

Offer guests a selection of alcoholic and non-alcoholic drinks. Don't forget to have low-calorie mixers for yourself and other slimmers.

Canapés can be very calorific. If you want to serve 'nibbles', prepare some crudités and low-calorie dips.

Make presentation a priority. The food *and* the table setting should both look inviting.

Minimise meal preparation time by choosing a cold starter and a cold dessert. For starters you could have melon balls and black grapes in port, pink grapefruit with prawns, or prawn cocktail with low-calorie seafood dressing. For dessert you could have fresh fruit salad, individual meringues topped with raspberries or other soft fruit, sorbet, low-calorie trifle, or low-calorie cheesecake.

Choose dishes that contrast in colour, texture and flavour. This sounds obvious, but it's a common mistake to combine dishes that are too similar to each other. For example, avoid serving a lemon mousse for dessert if you intend having a fish mousse starter.

Serve mineral water as well as wine with the meal so that drivers, slimmers and teetotallers are catered for.

Preparing Low-Calorie Dinner Parties
Starters

Choose	Avoid
melon	avocado
crudités	Anything fried/coated in oil-based dressings or
sorbet	mayonnaise
prawns	creamy soups

Main Courses

Choose	Avoid
poultry	anything fried
grilled { white fish	
{ lean meat	rich, creamy sauces
lobster	buttered vegetables
steamed vegetables	pastry dishes - pies and quiches
mixed salads dressed with yoghurt, lemon juice and herbs	batter or suet puddings

Desserts

Choose	*Avoid*
sorbet	fritters
fresh fruit	cream
unsweetened fruit salad	gateaux
fruit fools made with	pies/puddings
yoghurt, and no added sugar	
	meringues
...no dessert course!	
You will be surprised	choux pastry
how few of your guests	
will even notice	fruit fools made with
	custard and cream

Low Calorie Recipes

Here are some basic recipes which demonstrate the principles of making low-calorie versions of some favourite foods. Don't be afraid to experiment - you have nothing to lose but your excess weight.

...Coleslaw...

white cabbage
onion
low-calorie mayonnaise, oil-free dressing or low-calorie
seafood dressing
few drops lemon juice

Chop the cabbage and onion into thin shreds, either by hand or in a food processor. Mix in your chosen dressing and serve. For a change, try adding chopped carrot, celery, cucumber or cauliflower to the basic mixture — you'll soon find your favourite combination.

...Chicken risotto...

4 oz/125 g brown rice
4 oz/125 g frozen sweetcorn kernels
2 tsp polyunsaturated oil, or 1 tbsp water
1 small onion, chopped
1 small clove garlic, or 1 tsp garlic granules (optional)

1 tsp mild curry powder (optional)
14 oz/397 g tin tomatoes
few cauliflower or broccoli florets
6 oz/175 g cooked chicken

Boil the rice. When nearly done, boil the sweetcorn. Heat the oil or water in a non-stick pan and fry the onion until soft, not brown. Add the garlic and curry powder and cook over a gentle heat for a few minutes. Add the tomatoes, cauliflower, drained sweetcorn and chicken. Heat thoroughly for about 7 minutes, then stir in the rice. Serve with wholemeal bread.

...Chili casserole...

1 lb lean stewing beef, cut into 1 inch/2 cm cubes
1 medium onion, sliced
14 oz/397 g can red kidney beans, drained and rinsed
7 oz/200 g can low-sugar baked beans
1 tsp chilli powder
1 pint/285 ml beef stock

Heat the oven to gas mark 3/325 °F/170 °C. Place all the ingredients in a casserole. Cover and cook slowly for 2-2^1/$_2$ hours. Remove cover, strain off liquid and boil to reduce to desired consistency. Return to casserole and serve.

...Seafood dip...

5 oz/150 g low-fat natural yoghurt
3 level tbsp low-calorie seafood dressing
pinch pepper
1^1/$_2$ level tsp creamed horseradish (optional)

Combine all the ingredients by hand or in a food processor.

...Cheese, onion and garlic dip...

5 oz/150 g low-fat natural yoghurt
3 level tbsp low-calorie blue cheese dressing
3 oz/75 g chopped onion
1 clove garlic, crushed, or 2oz/50g chopped cucumber
(optional)

Combine all the ingredients by hand or in a food processor.

Variation: Use half yoghurt and half very low-fat fromage frais.

...Leanline lasagne...

(serves 4 — about 400 calories per serving)
12 oz/350 g lean or low-fat minced beef
1 tsp polyunsaturated oil or $^1/_2$ tsp water (optional)
1 medium onion, chopped
1 small green pepper, seeded and chopped
4 sticks celery, chopped
4 oz/125 g mushrooms, sliced
14 oz/397 g can tomatoes
2 cloves garlic, crushed, or 1 tsp garlic granules
$^1/_2$ tsp mixed herbs
$^1/_2$ tsp oregano
pinch cayenne pepper
1 stock cube, crumbled
4 oz/125 g wholewheat lasagne (no-pre-cooking variety)
1 oz/25 g cornflour
$^1/_2$ tsp mustard

pinch pepper
1 pint/568 ml skimmed milk
$1^1/_2$ oz/40 g Edam or low-fat hard cheese, grated

Brown the meat in a non-stick pan with or without the oil or water. Drain off any fat from the meat. Add the onion, green pepper, celery, mushrooms, tomatoes, garlic, herbs, cayenne and stock cube to the pan. Bring to the boil, then cover and simmer for 45 minutes, removing the lid for the last 10 minutes. Place half the meat mixture in an ovenproof dish and cover with half the lasagne. Repeat. Heat the oven to gas mark 6/400 °F/200 °C. Mix the cornflour, mustard and pepper with a little of the milk to form a smooth paste. Pour the remaining milk into a saucepan, stir in the cornflour paste and bring to the boil, stirring continuously. Cook gently for 1 minute. Stir in half the cheese. When melted, pour the sauce over the lasagne. Sprinkle the remaining cheese on top and bake for about 50 minutes.

Variation: Replace the meat with a mixture of vegetables, such as cauliflower, broccoli, carrots, sweetcorn, peas, leeks or kidney beans.

...Spirals with Lemon Sauce and Dill...

250 g/8 oz spirals
$^1/_4$ litre/8 fl oz milk
$^1/_8$ tsp salt
4 tbsp aquavit, or 4 tbsp vodka and 1 tsp caraway seeds
3 tbsp fresh lemon juice
5 cm/2 inch strip of lemon rind

2 tbsp finely cut fresh dill, or 2 tsp dried dill

Put the milk, salt, aquavit or vodka and caraway seeds, lemon juice and lemon rind in a large non-stick or heavy frying pan. Bring the liquid to the boil, reduce the heat and simmer gently for 3 minutes. Add the spirals and enough water to almost cover them. Cover the pan and cook over low heat, removing the lid and stirring occasionally, until the spirals are al dente and about 4 tablespoons of sauce remains—approximately 15 minutes. (If necessary, add more water to keep the spirals from sticking.) Remove the lemon rind and discard it. Stir in the chopped dill and serve the dish immediately.

...Spaghetti with Smoked Salmon and Watercress...

250 g/8 oz spaghetti
$1^1/_2$ tsp virgin olive oil
1 garlic clove, finely chopped
60 g/2 oz smoked salmon, julienned
1 bunch watercress, washed and stemmed
freshly ground black pepper

Cook the spaghetti in 3 litres (5 pints) of boiling water with $1^1/_2$ teaspoons of salt. Start testing the pasta after 8 minutes and cook it until it is *al dente*. Just before the spaghetti finishes cooking, heat the oil in a large frying pan over medium heat. Cook the garlic in the oil for 30 seconds, stirring constantly. Add the salmon, watercress and pepper, and cook for 30 seconds more before removing the pan from the heat. Drain the spaghetti and add it to the pan. Toss the spaghetti to distribute the sauce and serve at once.

...Courgette Tian...

750 g/1¹/₂ lb courgettes, trimmed and finely sliced
3 tsp virgin olive oil
60 g/2 oz brown rice
1 garlic clove
¹/₄ tsp salt
3 shallots, finely chopped
2 small eggs, beaten
2 tbsp freshly grated Parmesan cheese
1 tbsp shredded fresh rocket leaves
1 tbsp shredded fresh basil leaves
1 tbsp finely chopped flat-leaf parsley
¹/₈ tsp white pepper

Place the courgettes in a heavy-bottomed saucepan with 2 teaspoons of the oil and cook them gently over low heat, covered, until they are just tender—about 10 minutes. Stir from time to time to prevent the courgettes from sticking.

Meanwhile, rinse the brown rice under cold running water and place it in a small, heavy-bottomed saucepan with 30 cl (¹/₂ pint) of water. Bring the water to the boil, then reduce the heat, cover the pan and simmer for 15 minutes. Drain the rice well and set it aside, covered.

Preheat the oven to 180 °C (350 °F or Mark 4). Crush the garlic with the salt. Heat the remaining teaspoon of oil in a small, heavy-bottomed saucepan, add the shallots and garlic, and soften them over very low heat, covered, for about 5 minutes.

Lightly grease a wide, shallow gratin dish. In a large mixing bowl, stir together the courgettes, rice, shallots and garlic; add the eggs and half of the Parmesan. Stir well, then mix in the rocket, basil, parsley and pepper. Transfer the mixture to the prepared dish, levelling the courgette slices so that they lie flat, and sprinkle on the remaining Parmesan.

Bake the tian in the oven, uncovered, for 20 minutes, then increase the oven temperature to 220 °C (425 °F or Mark 7) and bake it for a further 10 to 15 minutes, until a crust has formed.

Serve hot or warm.

...Red-Cooked Beef...

1 kg/2 lb topside of beef, trimmed of fat and cut into 2 cm ($^3/_4$ inch) pieces

4 Chinese dried mushrooms, soaked in hot water for 10 to 15 minutes

3 tbsp low-sodium soy sauce or shoyu

2 tbsp dry sherry

2 tbsp soft brown sugar

1 tbsp tomato paste

2.5 cm/1 inch fresh ginger root, peeled and crushed

2 garlic cloves, crushed

1/2 tsp five-spice powder

$^1/_4$ litre/8 fl oz unsalted brown stock

1 tbsp safflower oil

300 g/10 oz carrots, thinly sliced diagonally

Drain the mushrooms and gently squeeze out excess moisture. Trim and slice them. Place them in a bowl with the soy sauce or shoyu, sherry, brown sugar, tomato paste, ginger, garlic, five-spice powder and stock. Stir well and set aside.

Heat the oil in a heavy fireproof casserole over high heat. Add one third of the beef pieces and brown them on all sides, turning them constantly—about 5 minutes. With a slotted spoon, drain the meat, then transfer it to a plate lined with paper towels. Repeat with the remaining two batches of beef, draining each batch on fresh towels. Return all the beef to the casserole, add the mushrooms and liquid mixture and bring slowly to the boil Reduce the heat, cover and simmer very gently for 1 1/2 hours, turning the meat over frequently during this time and basting with the cooking liquid.

Add the carrots and continue cooking for a further 30 minutes or until the beef is tender; the carrots should be cooked but still firm. Serve hot.

...Braised Chicken with Plums and Lemons...

4 chicken breasts, skinned and boned (about 500 g/1 Ib)
$^1/_2$ litre/16 fl oz unsalted chicken stock
4 red plums, blanched in the stock for 1 minute, peeled
(skins reserved), halved and stoned
2 tsp sugar
30 g/1 oz unsalted butter
$^1/_8$ tsp salt
freshly ground black pepper
2 tbsp chopped shallots

8 paper-thin lemon slices

In a saucepan over medium heat, cook the plum skins in the chicken stock until the liquid is reduced to 12.5 cl (4 fl oz).

Strain the stock and return it to the pan. Reduce the heat to low, and add the plum halves and sugar. Simmer the mixture for 1 minute, then remove it from the heat and set aside. Preheat the oven to 190 °C (375 °F or Mark 5).

In a shallow fireproof casserole over medium heat, melt the butter. Lay the breasts in the casserole and sauté them lightly on one side for about 2 minutes. Turn them over, salt and pepper the cooked side, and add the shallots. Place the plum halves cut side down between the breasts. Pour the stock into the casserole and arrange two lemon slices on each breast.

Put the uncovered casserole in the oven. Cook until the chicken feels firm but springy to the touch—about 10 minutes. Remove the casserole from the oven and lift out the plums and breasts with a slotted spoon Place them on a warmed platter and return the lemon slices to the sauce. Cover the chicken and plums with foil to keep them warm. Simmer the sauce over medium-high heat until it is reduced to about 4 tablespoons—5 to 7 minutes. Put the lemon slices back on top of the breasts and arrange the plums around them. Pour the sauce over all and serve.

...Honey-Basil Chicken...

4 whole chicken legs, skinned
$\frac{1}{4}$ tsp salt
freshly ground black pepper
1 tbsp safflower oil
7.5 g/$\frac{1}{4}$ oz unsalted butter
2 tbsp honey
2 tbsp unsalted chicken stock

2 garlic cloves, thinly sliced
30 to 40 fresh basil leaves

Preheat the oven to 200 °C (400 °F or Mark 6). Cut a piece of aluminium foil 30 cm (1 ft) square for each leg. Sprinkle the legs with the salt and pepper. Heat the oil and butter in a frying pan over medium heat, then brown the legs for about 2 minutes on each side. Put a leg in the middle of each foil square, and dribble $1^1/_2$ teaspoons of the honey and $1^1/_2$ teaspoons of the stock over each one. Lay one quarter of the garlic slices on each piece, cover with a loose layer of the basil leaves, and wrap the foil snugly over the top. Put the foil packages on a baking sheet and set it in the oven.

After 30 minutes, remove a foil package from the oven and unwrap it carefully to preserve the juices. Test for doneness by piercing the thigh with the tip of a sharp knife; if the juices run clear, it is done. If necessary, return the leg to the oven and bake about 5 minutes more.

To serve, undo each package and transfer the legs to a platter. Remove any garlic or basil that sticks to the foil and put them back on the chicken. Pour the collected juices from the foil packages over the legs.

...Red Pepper Pork with Mint...

500 g/1 lb pork fillet or loin, trimmed of fat and thinly sliced
1 tbsp virgin olive oil
2 sweet red peppers, seeded, deribbed and thinly sliced
freshly ground black pepper
500 g/1 lb tomatoes, skinned, seeded and chopped

$^1/_4$ tsp salt
2 tbsp finely chopped fresh mint
45 g/1$^1/_2$ oz fromage frais (optional)

Heat the oil in a heavy frying pan; add the red peppers and sauté for 1 minute. Add the pork slices and brown them over high heat. Season with some black pepper, then cover the pan and reduce the heat to low. After 5 minutes, add the tomatoes; continue to cook, covered, for 10 to 15 minutes, or until the meat is tender and the tomato-pepper mixture is well reduced. Season with the salt and some more pepper, if required.

Remove the pan from the heat and leave it to cool for 1 minute, then stir in the mint and, if you are using it, the fromage frais. Serve at once.

...Pork Char-Shiu...

2 pork fillets (about 300 g/10 oz each), thin ends cut off, trimmed of fat
2 tbsp low-sodium soy sauce or shoyu
3 or 4 spring onions, finely chopped
2.5 cm/1 inch piece fresh ginger root, finely chopped
2 garlic cloves, finely chopped
$^1/_2$ tsp Sichuan pepper
2 star anise
1 tbsp dry sherry
1 tbsp honey
1$^1/_2$ tsp red wine vinegar
$^1/_2$ tsp cornflour or potato flour, mixed with 2 tbsp water
mixed salad leaves, washed and dried

Rub the pork with 1 tablespoon of the soy sauce and leave for 20 minutes in a cool place. In a mortar, pound the spring onions, ginger and garlic to a rough paste with the Sichuan pepper and star anise. Mix in the sherry, the remaining soy sauce, half of the honey and 1 teaspoon of the vinegar; coat the pork with the paste and leave it to marinate for 2 to 6 hours in the refrigerator, turning it once or twice.

Remove the pork from the refrigerator, pat it dry with paper towels and discard any dry ingredients that are sticking to it. Strain the marinade and reserve. Prepare a glazing syrup by mixing 1 teaspoon of hot water with the remaining honey and vinegar.

Preheat the grill to very hot, place the meat close to the source of heat and brown it on both sides for 3 to 4 minutes. Move the meat to about 10 cm (4 inches) from the heat source and continue to cook for a further 10 minutes, turning a few times and basting constantly with the glazing syrup. Test for doneness with a skewer—the juice that runs out should be almost clear. Cover the cooked fillet loosely with aluminium foil, and leave to rest for 5 minutes.

Heat the reserved marinade to a simmer, add the cornflour or potato flour mixture and bring back to simmer. To serve, cut the fillet across the grain into thin slices and place them on a bed of salad leaves. Serve the marinade separately as a dipping sauce.

...Turkey Crust Pizza...

1 kg/2 lb white and dark turkey meat, skinned, minced or finely chopped

45 g/1$^1/_2$ oz dry breadcrumbs
1 spring onion, chopped
2 egg whites, lightly beaten
4 drops Tabasco sauce
2 tsp virgin olive oil
$^1/_4$ tsp salt
freshly ground black pepper
2 tbsp white wine
150 g/5 oz grated low-fat mozzarella and Gruyere cheese,
combined

Pizza sauce

1 tbsp virgin olive oil
90 g/3 oz onion, finely chopped
1 large sweet green or red pepper, halved, seeded, deribbed,
cut into narrow strips
135 g/4$^1/_2$ oz thinly sliced mushrooms
1 kg/35 oz canned Italian whole plum tomatoes
2 large garlic cloves, finely chopped
2 tbsp red wine vinegar
2 tsp sugar
1 tbsp chopped fresh basil, or 1 tsp dried basil
$^1/_2$ tsp dried oregano
$^1/_4$ tsp salt
freshly ground black pepper

To make the sauce, place the oil in a heavy-bottomed saucepan over medium-low heat, and cook the onion for 3 minutes,
stirring frequently. Add the pepper strips and mushrooms and
cook for 2 minutes. Add the rest of the sauce ingredients. Bring
to the boil, reduce the heat and simmer gently for 40 minutes,

stirring occasionally.

Preheat the oven to 200 °C (400 °F or Mark 6). Combine the breadcrumbs, spring onion, egg whites, Tabasco sauce, 1 teaspoon of the oil, and the salt and pepper in a large bowl. Add 12.5 cl (4 fl oz) of the pizza sauce and the white wine. Mix in the minced turkey.

Rub a shallow 25 to 30 cm (10 to 12 inch) round baking dish with the remaining teaspoon of oil. Spread the turkey mixture evenly over the bottom of the dish, pushing it up all round the sides to resemble a crust. Pour half of the warm sauce on to the turkey crust Cover with the grated cheeses. Ladle the remaining sauce over the cheese layer. Sprinkle with freshly ground black pepper. Place the dish on the upper level of the oven and bake for 15 minutes. Remove and let stand for 5 minutes. Cut in wedges and serve immediately.

...Fatless sponge...

2 eggs
3oz/75g caster sugar
3oz/75g self-raising flour

Heat the oven to gas mark 4/350 °F/170 °C. Break the eggs into a bowl, whisk lightly and add the sugar. Whisk again until thick and creamy. Sieve the flour and fold into the mixture. Pour into a 7 inch/18 cm cake tin. Bake for about 30 minutes. When cooked, slice in half and sandwich together with low-sugar jam, or low-fat yoghurt and sliced fresh fruit, such as pineapple.

...Low-fat ice-cream...

(makes 1½ pints/900 ml)
1 diabetic jelly, same flavour as yoghurt
1½ pints/900 ml low-fat fruit yoghurt
1 egg, separated
3 tbsp skimmed milk powder mixed with ½ pint/285 ml
water

Mix the jelly crystals with a little water in a heatproof bowl. Place over a pan of hot water and stir until dissolved. Leave to cool slightly, then stir in the yoghurt. Whisk the egg yolk until pale, then beat into the yoghurt mixture. Beat in the milk. Pour the mixture into a freezer tray and freeze for about 25 minutes. Remove and beat well. Whisk the egg white until stiff, then fold into the mixture. Return to the freezer tray and freeze until firm.

Note: You can make a low-calorie version of any ice-cream recipe by simply using low-fat yoghurt instead of cream.

Eating Out

Many slimmers find that eating out is a great challenge to their dieting. Whether you are eating out for business or pleasure, there are five main ways to approach the situation.

1 Forget about the diet altogether.

This may work for those who eat out *rarely*. The occasional over-indulgence should not ruin your slimming, as long as the diet is resumed immediately.

2 Stick to your diet rules.

This is obviously effective — if you have the self-control to do it, If so, congratulations, and carry on.

3 Indulge and balance.

Indulge on a moderate, planned scale, and 'balance' by reducing your calorie intake the day before and the day after the meal. This is effective if it is planned and strictly adhered to. Remember that restaurants often increase the calorie content of food by their methods of preparation, such as frying meat, adding cream to sauces, using oily salad dressings. Take this into account when 'balancing' your calories.

4 Eat a little of everything that you really like.

This is effective if 'a little' really is only 'a little'.

5 Eat the lowest-calorie choices available.

This is a useful system. Learn which are the lower calorie dishes. Remember as the customer you are entitled to ask the chef to provide plainly-cooked versions of meat, fish or vegetables.

Choose the method that works best for you and try to avoid restaurants that do not cater for your needs. Many restaurant owners are happy to oblige, if asked, but many slimmers use eating out as an excuse to over-indulge.

If you have regular business meals, try to frequent a particular establishment that will be more responsive to your needs.

When eating out, don't forget that it is also essential to limit alcohol intake. An aperitif and a glass of wine can make a big dent in your calorie allowance.

Finally, try to regard the occasions and the company as the main pleasures, rather than the food.

Parties

Party-time can be danger-time when you are dieting. A bountiful buffet table is designed to tempt you into overeating, and the dishes are often more calorific than they appear. However the tips below will help you survive whether you are giving or going to a party.

Do not starve yourself all day before a party; you will be so hungry that you might binge.

Have a day of light eating the day before and the day after the party.

Decide beforehand whether you will indulge in alcohol, and if so, how much. (Too much alcohol can lead to too much eating)

Make 'shorts' into long drinks by adding low-calorie mixers. Also add soda water to wine to make a 'spritzer'.

Dance as much as possible; it's enjoyable, uses up calories and minimises time for food and drink.

Eat less of your favourite foods. but don't cut them out entirely.

Don't eat something of everything just for the sake of it.

Focus on the company and socialising rather than on the food.

...Giving a party?

Avoid serving sausage rolls, vol-au-vents and sausages on sticks; they're boring and very fattening.

Serve visually appealing food, such as tiny rolled-up sandwiches, rolled-up lean meats, and colourful rice salads.

Offer low-calorie alternatives wherever possible.

Provide low-calorie dips with fresh vegetable crudités instead of nuts and crisps.

Set aside a plate of carefully chosen low-calorie food for yourself beforehand, then eat no more.

Have low-calorie mixers available, at least for yourself.

Put food and drink in a separate room from the dancing and socialising — it's less tempting.

...Going to a party?

Take low-calorie mixers with you.

Choose lower-calorie food, and don't feel deprived.

Allow yourself only one serving; leave seconds to others .

Whatever the occasion, enjoy making the most of your slimmer appearance, and remember that you *can* enjoy yourself without overeating.

The Demon Drink

The words of the song say, 'Another little drink won't do you any harm', but is this really so?

The wise slimmer is aiming not only to reduce excess weight, but also to discover fitness and health.

Of all social habits, drinking alcohol is probably the most difficult to curb. Excess weight is normally associated with food, but alcohol is relatively high in calories and can make big inroads to your daily calorie allowance.

No one denies that alcohol can make you feel good, but it contains no nutrients, so it has no food value. Consequently, it is possible for a heavy drinker to be fat, yet still suffer from malnutrition.

Alcohol is sometimes referred to as 'intoxicating liquor', and the word 'toxic' should remind us of its poisonous effects on the body; aggression and violence in the short term, but liver damage, ulcers, high blood pressure, depression, sexual difficulties and brain damage in the long term.

...How much is too much?

Recent research by the Health Education Authority indicates that it is safe to drink, provided you keep within recommended guidelines. Alcohol is measured in units, one unit being equal to $1/2$ pint/250 ml ordinary strength beer, or one single pub measure of spirits, sherry, wine or vermouth. The recommended weekly allowance is 21 units for men and 14 units for women (female physiology does not allow equality!).

Apart from alcohol's high calorie content, it can have other drawbacks for slimmers. Firstly, it takes effect more quickly because of your reduced food intake; secondly, it impairs judgement, so many a slimmer succumbs to overeating while under the influence; thirdly, the subsequent hangover may lead to consoling yourself with unnecessary food.

If you can, try to exclude alcohol from your diet completely. This may be difficult, especially as alcohol is such a part of the social fabric. However, many people have succeeded in changing their drinking habits, not least because of the impact of 'drink-driving' campaigns.

If you can't give up alcohol, keep your consumption in check and don't be tempted to 'save' your units for a once or twice-weekly binge. The following tips might help you to reduce your intake.

• 'Home measures' are usually more generous than 'pub measures', so take account of this when calculating your intake.

• 'Low alcohol' does not mean 'low calorie'. Consult a calorie list.

• 'Lengthen' your alcoholic drink by adding soda water or low-calorie mixers.

• Finish one measure of alcohol at a time. Topping up makes it difficult to calculate your intake.

• Pace your alcohol intake throughout an evening and do not get involved in buying rounds.

• Plan alcohol-free days each week, and stick to them. This is frequently more successful than making a vague resolve to cut down.

• Say 'no' firmly — not in a way that encourages persuasion.

• If saying no is difficult, take assertion classes or read up about assertion techniques (see 'Further Reading').

• If you are dependent on alcohol, seek expert advice (see 'Useful Addresses').

Setting Personal Targets

Target setting is used successfully in business to improve results. It is based on the principle that if you take time to propose a specific goal and write it down, you are more likely to achieve it than if it remains a vague idea in your mind.

This is also a useful technique for the slimmer because it focuses attention on the weight to be lost in a set period of time. Perhaps, for example, you wish to lose weight for Christmas, a holiday, or a special occasion, such as a wedding.

• Think ahead. Six weeks is a practical time-period.

• Choose the amount of weight you aim to lose in the period. Set realistic targets so you can sustain motivation. Aim to lose an average of 2 lb/1 kg per week, perhaps even a little less. Unrealistic targets simply promote failure and disappointment.

• Weigh yourself at the beginning of your diet and keep a personal record. Each week, reweigh yourself and fill in the details.

• Periodically review your progress towards your target. If you are progressing well, don't use it as an excuse to over-indulge. If you are not making much headway, don't despair Review your eating for the week, locate your mistakes and work out how to avoid them next week.

Rewarding Yourself

Many people, especially women, are reluctant to reward themselves. They find it relatively easy to reward others — family, children and employees — but for various, sometimes complex, reasons, they do not extend the same consideration towards themselves. This pattern must be broken if you are to succeed in a long-term task like slimming. In fact, it is essential to build in rewards to sustain your efforts.

Before you jump to conclusions, don't think that rewards necessarily mean food. As children, most of us were given something nice to eat to take away the taste of nasty medicine, to console us after a fall, or to congratulate us on passing exams. Consequently, we become conditioned to regard food as reward. This is unhelpful and potentially destructive thinking which the slimmer especially must abandon. How can you do this?

• Stop giving yourself food as a reward. If this is difficult at first, allow yourself 'quality' foods, such as smoked salmon or prawns, rather than the confectionery and sugary treats of your childhood.

• Make a list of the alternatives that could be rewards for you — perhaps a massage or Turkish bath, a professional make-up session, some new clothes, perfume, glossy magazines, coveted records or books. Perhaps you'd like the reward to be spending time by yourself — walking, resting, or even in the bath. Maybe you could make a trip to the theatre or cinema with a friend, or organise a babysitter so you can spend extra time alone with your partner.

- Plan your rewards in advance and enjoy anticipating them.
- Mark the successful milestones of your weight-loss, say, each 7 lb/3 kg, with a reward.

Once you've earned your reward, revel in it — you deserve it!

Exercise: Why Bother?

It *is* possible to lose weight without exercising, but slimming is faster and more effective with exercise. Why? Obviously, exercise uses up calories, but it is now thought that there are many extra benefits.

• Metabolism is speeded up—an effect that lasts — so that, after the exercise session, extra calories continue to be used up.

• Muscle develops — the body becomes more shapely, with less flab.

• A muscle-developed body burns up more calories than a 'flabby' body of the same weight.

• Exercise raises the spirits by causing the brain to release mood-lifting hormones — your own natural anti-depressant.

• Physical fitness is enhanced, so you have more energy and stamina.

• Suppleness develops, which makes general movement easier and the body less prone to strains.

...What sort of exercise?

Almost any exercise is better than none. For maximum benefit, exercise should be:

- Aerobic
- At least 20 minutes continuously (after warm-up)
- 3-4 times per week

Aerobic exercises always involve having both feet off the ground at some point. They include running, skiing, rowing, cycling, swimming, energetic dancing and brisk walking (with vigorous arm-swings).

Low-impact aerobic exercise is a fairly new development, designed to minimise injury to joints and muscles. It involves keeping one foot on the ground at all times.

For exercise to be aerobic it must raise the heart-rate to within 60-75 per cent of its maximum, as measured by your pulse. Your recommended maximum heart-rate can be calculated by subtracting your age from 220 and then calculating 60-75 per cent of that figure. For example, a person 35 years old would make the following sum:

$$220 - 35 = 185$$
$$185 \times 60\% = 111$$
$$185 \times 75\% = 139$$

The target zone for this person's pulse rate is between 111 and 139.

To take your pulse, locate the beat at your wrist with two fingers of one hand. Count the number of beats for 15 seconds. Multiply this number by four to obtain the number of beats per minute.

Alternatively, you could buy a pulse-meter, a wristwatch-style device with a monitoring attachment that fastens to a finger or ear. These are available from sports shops.

...Starting an exercise programme

Note the following points before you contemplate any kind of exercise:

• Consult your doctor first if you are very unfit, more than $1^1/_2$ stones/9.5 kg overweight, have any medical condition or are over 40 years old.

• Ease into your exercise programme; too much can be more damaging than too little.

• Start by walking 15 minutes a day, four times a week. Increase your speed and time sensibly each week, according to your fitness level.

• Swimming is excellent exercise, whatever your age, and is probably the best choice for those who are very overweight. Join a class if you can't swim. Many pools open early so people can swim before going to work.

• When your fitness level and weight allow, choose other aerobic activities. Walking, running and cycling clubs welcome beginners and the group effort enhances motivation. Alternatively, join an exercise class.

...Choosing a class

Whatever kind of exercise class you take, do ensure that it is run by a qualified and experienced teacher who regularly checks your performance. Avoid classes which have too many members to allow proper supervision.

...Home exercise

If you prefer to exercise in private, buy an exercise bike and gradually build up to 20 minute sessions. Move through the gears until you are pedalling as hard as possible. To alleviate the boredom of this exercise, read, listen to music or watch television.

Other items of home exercise equipment, such as a rowing machine, mini-trampoline, weights or jogging 'treadmill' can be purchased for your home 'gym', if you have enough space and enthusiasm.

Less bulky are the many exercise programmes available on video and audio cassettes. Make sure you do warm-up exercises first and always follow the instructions.

It is all too easy to find excuses for not exercising, especially if you have to juggle work and home commitments. Even if you find it difficult to set time aside for exercise sessions, you can still build activity into your day. For example, use the stairs rather than lifts or escalators, and walk short distances that you usually drive.

The benefits of exercise take a while to show, but your efforts will be rewarded with a fitter, slimmer you.

Staying Slim

So, you have reached the ideal/target weight you have set your-self — congratulations!

Now begins the time that many slimmers believe is even more difficult — preventing that excess weight from piling back on.

You have practised new eating habits while on your diet, and now you have lost weight, it is easy to think that you are off the diet and can go back to your old ways of eating. This is a mistake. Your old ways of eating were actually ways of overeating, and were the cause of your excess weight.

...How to stay slim

• Continue to practise your slim-cooking habits.

• Continue to eat low-fat, no added-sugar substitutes.

• Continue to 'think slim'.

• Continue to exercise.

• Allow yourself a few extra calories a day, say, 100 to begin with, and check that your weight is remaining stable. If not, adjust the extra calories accordingly. You could 'save' the ex-tra calories for a weekend treat.

• Weigh yourself once each week. Don't forget that if you weigh after an indulgent weekend, the extra carbohydrates and sugar will cause some water retention and the weight gain may be more than expected. A stricter weekday routine will soon correct this.

• It may be more realistic to think of staying within a suitable weight range, rather than at an exact weight. This allows for premenstrual gains and holiday or seasonal gains.

• As soon as you reach those few pounds above your ideal, apply your slimming principles strictly to reduce the excess.

• Do not crash diet.

• Take note of how your clothes fit. If they start to feel tight, begin your slimming principles immediately — and strictly.

• Don't panic about weight gain. You have learned how to lose weight successfully, so you can do it again, if necessary.

• After the congratulations about your weight-loss have died down, you must constantly remind yourself how much better you look and feel in your slim body. Never allow yourself to forget the disadvantages of being overweight, and then you will not allow yourself to slip back into the bad habits that made you fat.

Further Reading

...Cookery

Bloomsbury Kitchen Library,
(Bloomsbury Books, 1994)

Cooking for Your Heart's Content,
British Heart Foundation (Arrow, 1978)

The Cook's Handbook,
Prue Leith (Macmillan, 1981)

Cooking with Herbs and Spices,
Good Housekeeping Institute (Ebury Press, 1975)

Cooking with Herbs and Spices,
Jill Graham (Reed, 1984)

Creative Steam Cuisine,
Kate Benson (Hamlyn, 1988)

The Healthy Gourmet Cookbook,
Barbara Bassett (Arlington, 1985)

Healthy Home Cooking
(Time Life, 1986)

Home Cooking
(Time Life/Geddes & Grosset, 1994)

Low-Fat and No-Fat Cookbook,
Jackie Applebee (Thorsons, 1984)

Low-Fat Cookery,
Wendy Godfrey(Sainsbury, 1985)

Slim and Fit Family Cookbook,
Good Housekeeping Institute (Ebury Press, 1982)

The Slim Gourmet Cookbook,
Barbara Gibbons (Harper & Row, 1976)

Slimmers' Microwave Cookbook,
Margaret Weale (David & Charles, 1983)

Slimming Menus,
Audrey Ellis (Sampson Low, 1979)

...Depression and Street

Beating Depression,
Dr John Rush (Century, 1983)

Depression: The Way Out of our Prison,
Dorothy Rowe (Routledge & Kegan Paul, 1983)

Stress and Relaxation,
Jane Madders (Martin Dunitz, 1980)

Stressmanship,
Audrey Livingstone-Booth (Severn House, 1985)

...Eating Disorders

Anorexia Nervosa: *Let Me Be*,
A.H. Crisp (Academic Press, 1980)

The Art of Starvation,
Sheila Macleod (Virago, 1981)

Bulimarexia,
M. Boskind-White and WC. White (Norton, 1983)

Coping with Bulimia,
Barbara French (Thorsons, 1987)

Feasting and Fasting,
Paulette Maisner (Fontant, 1985)

Hunger Strike,
Susie Orbach (Faber, 1986)

Useful Addresses

Al-Anon Family Groups
61 Great Dover Street,
London SEI 4YF
Tel: 071-403 0888
Offers advice and support to the families and partners of those
with alcohol problems.

Alcoholics Anonymous
11 Redcliffe Gardens, London
SW10 9GB
Tel: 071-352 3001
Support and advice for those dependent on alcohol.

Anorexic Family Aid
Sackville Place,44 Magdalen Street,
Norwich, Norfolk NJ3 IJE
Tel: (0603) 621414
Advice and support for anorexics, bulimics and their families.

Health Education Authority
78 New Oxford Street,
London WC1A 1AH
Tel: 071-383 3833

Free leaflets on healthy eating, exercise, smoking, alcohol and all other aspects of health. Alternatively, contact your local Health Education Unit, listed in the phone book under your district health authority. Nationwide classes are available under the auspices of the HEA — contact:

Look After Yourself Project Centre
Christ Church College,
Canterbury, Kent CT1 1QU
Tel: (0227) 455687

The Maisner Centre for Eating Disorders
PO Box 464, Hove,
East Sussex BN3 2BN
Tel: (0273) 729818
Supportive and sympathetic help for anorexics and compulsive eaters of both sexes and all ages.

Premenstrual Tension Advisory Service
PO Box 268, Hove,
East Sussex BN3 1RW
Tel: (0273) 487366

Relate (formerly Marriage Guidance Council)
Little Church Street,
Rugby
Tel: (0788) 565675
Free and confidential help for those with sexual or emotional difficulties within relationships.

Relaxation for Living
29 Burnwood Park Road,
Walton-on-Thames,
Surrey KT12 5LH
Tel: (0932) 227826
Nationwide classes and correspondence courses on relaxation
techniques. Free information booklet available by sending a
SAE to 168/170 Oatland Drive, Weighbridge, Surrey,
KT13 9ET.

Well Woman Clinic
Marie Stopes House,
108 Whitfield Street, London W1
Tel: 071-388 2585
Advice on all aspects of women's health.

Calories

The tables in this book give figures for calories (KCALS)—measurements of the energy value of foods. Calorie-counting is popular as a method of dieting with the individual following a programme of perhaps 1,500 calories per day, or 1,000 calories per day, according to advice.

Figures are also given for carbohydrate, protein and fat content measured in grams. This makes the book useful to those who have chosen, or have been advised to follow a low-fat or low-carbohydrate diet, or who wish to monitor their protein intake.

FRUIT

SPECIFIC	AMOUNT	KCALS	CARB	PROT	FAT
Apples					
cooking, raw, peeled	100g	35	8.9	0.3	0.1
cooking, stewed with sugar	100g	74	19.1	0.3	0.1
cooking, stewed with sugar	1 portion [140g]	103	26.7	0.4	0.1
cooking, stewed without sugar	100g	33	8.1	0.3	0.1
cooking, stewed without sugar	1 portion [140g]	46	11.3	0.4	0.1
eating, raw, weighed without core	100g	47	11.8	0.4	0.1
eating, raw, with core	100g	42	10.5	0.4	0.1
eating, raw, with core	1 small [75g]	32	7.9	0.3	0.1
eating, raw, with core	1 medium [112g]	47	11.8	0.4	0.1
eating, raw, with core	1 large [170g]	71	17.9	0.7	0.2
eating, raw, peeled	100g	45	11.2	0.4	0.1
Apricots					
canned in juice	100g	34	8.4	0.5	0.1
canned in juice	1 portion [140g]	48	11.8	0.7	0.1
canned in syrup	100g	63	16.1	0.4	0.1
canned in syrup	1 portion [140g]	88	22.5	0.6	0.1
raw, without stone	100g	31	8.5	0.3	0.1
raw, without stone	1 [65g]	20	5.5	0.2	0.1

103

SPECIFIC	AMOUNT	KCALS	CARB	PROT	FAT
semi-dried, ready-to-eat	100g	158	36.5	4.0	0.6
Avocado					
raw, without skin or stone	100g	190	1.9	1.9	19.5
raw, without skin or stone	1 small [100g]	190	1.9	1.9	19.5
raw, without skin or stone	1 medium [145]	275	2.8	2.8	28.3
raw, without skin or stone	1 large [195g]	371	3.7	3.7	38.0
Banana					
with skin	100g	95	23.2	1.2	0.3
with skin	1 small [130g]	123	30.2	1.6	0.4
with skin	1 medium [150g]	143	34.8	1.8	0.5
with skin	1 large [180g]	171	41.8	2.2	0.5
Blackberries					
raw	100g	62	15.3	0.8	0.2
stewed with sugar	100g	56	13.8	0.7	0.2
stewed with sugar	1 portion [140g]	78	19.3	1.0	0.3
stewed without sugar	100g	21	4.4	0.8	0.2
stewed withour sugar	1 portion [140g]	29	6.2	1.1	0.3
Blackcurrants					
canned in juice	100g	31	7.6	0.8	trace

SPECIFIC	AMOUNT	KCALS	CARB	PROT	FAT
canned in syrup	100g	72	18.4	0.7	trace
raw	100g	28	6.6	0.9	trace
stewed with sugar	100g	58	15.0	0.7	trace
stewed with sugar	1 portion [140g]	81	21.0	1.0	trace
Cherries					
canned in syrup	100g	71	18.5	0.5	trace
cherries, glace	100g	251	66.4	0.4	trace
raw, without stone	100g	48	11.5	0.9	0.1
raw, without stone	1 [10g]	5	0.6	trace	trace
Cherry pie filling	100g	82	21.5	0.4	trace
Clementines					
raw, without skin	100g	37	8.7	0.9	0.1
raw, without skin	1 small [40g]	15	3.5	0.4	trace
raw, without skin	1 medium [60g]	22	5.2	0.5	0.1
raw, without skin	1 large [80g]	30	7.0	0.7	0.1
Currants	100g	267	67.8	2.3	0.4
Damsons					
raw, without stones	100g	34	8.6	0.5	trace

Specific	Amount	Kcals	Carb	Prot	Fat
raw, without stones	1 [15g]	5	1.3	trace	trace
stewed with sugar	100g	74	19.3	0.4	trace
stewed with sugar	1 portion [140g]	104	27.0	0.6	trace
Dates					
dried, with stones	100g	227	57.1	2.8	0.2
dried, with stone	1 [20g]	45	11.4	0.6	trace
raw, with stones	100g	107	26.9	1.3	0.1
raw, with stone	1 [30g]	32	8.1	0.4	trace
Figs					
dried	100g	227	52.9	3.6	1.6
dried	1 [20g]	45	10.6	0.7	0.3
semi-dried, ready-to-eat	100g	209	48.6	3.3	1.5
semi-dried, ready-to-eat	1 [35g]	73	17.0	1.2	0.5
Fruit pie filling					
average	100g	77	20.1	0.4	trace
Fruit cocktail					
canned in juice	100g	29	7.2	0.4	trace
canned in juice	1 portion [105g]	30	7.6	0.4	trace
canned in syrup	100g	57	14.8	0.4	trace

Specific	Amount	Kcals	Carb	Prot	Fat
canned in syrup	1 portion [105g]	60	15.5	0.4	trace
Fruit salad					
home made [bananas, oranges, apples, pears and grapes]	100g	55	13.8	0.7	0.1
home made [bananas, oranges, apples, pears and grapes]	1 portion [140g]	77	19.3	1.0	0.1
Gooseberries					
cooking, raw	100g	19	3.0	1.1	0.4
dessert, canned in syrup	100g	73	18.5	0.4	0.2
dessert, canned in syrup	1 portion [105g]	77	19.4	0.4	0.2
stewed with sugar	100g	54	12.9	0.7	0.3
stewed with sugar	1portion [140g]	76	2.7	1.0	0.4
stewed without sugar	100g	16	2.5	0.9	0.3
stewed without sugar	1 portion [140g]	22	3.5	1.3	0.4
Grapefruit					
canned in juice	100g	30	7.3	0.6	trace
canned in juice	1 portion [105g]	32	7.7	0.6	trace
canned in syrup	100g	60	15.5	0.5	trace
canned in syrup	1 portion [105g]	63	16.3	0.5	trace
raw, with skin	100g	20	4.6	0.5	0.1

SPECIFIC	AMOUNT	KCALS	CARB	PROT	FAT
raw, with skin	1 small [250g]	50	11.5	1.3	0.3
raw, with skin	1 medium [340g]	68	15.6	1.7	0.3
raw, with skin	1 large [425g]	85	19.6	2.1	0.4
Grapes					
raw, black and white	100g	60	15.4	0.4	0.1
raw, black and white	1 [5g]	3	0.8	trace	trace
Guava					
canned in syrup	100g	60	15.7	0.4	trace
canned in syrup	1 portion [105g]	63	16.5	0.4	trace
raw	100g	26	5.0	0.8	0.5
Kiwi fruit					
raw, without skin	100g	49	10.6	1.1	0.5
raw, without skin	1 [60g]	29	6.3	0.7	0.3
Lemons					
raw, with peel	100g	19	3.2	1.0	0.3
raw, with peel	1 medium [125g]	24	4.0	1.3	0.3
Lychees					
canned in syrup	100g	68	17.7	0.4	trace

SPECIFIC	AMOUNT	KCALS	CARB	PROT	FAT
canned in syrup	1 portion [105g]	71	18.6	0.4	trace
raw, without stone	100g	58	14.3	0.9	0.1
raw, without stone	1 [15g]	9	2.1	0.1	trace
Mandarin oranges					
canned in juice	100g	32	7.7	0.7	trace
canned in juice	1 portion [105g]	34	8.1	0.7	trace
canned in syrup	100g	52	13.4	0.5	trace
canned in syrup	1 portion [105g]	55	14.1	0.5	trace
Mangoes					
canned in syrup	100g	77	20.3	0.3	trace
canned in syrup	1 portion [105g]	81	21.3	0.3	trace
raw, without stone or skin	100g	57	14.1	0.7	0.2
raw, without stone or skin	1 slice [40g]	23	5.6	0.3	trace
Melon					
Canteloupe, without skin or seeds	100g	19	4.2	0.6	0.1
Canteloupe, without skin or seeds	1 slice [150g]	29	6.3	0.9	0.2
Galia, without skin or seeds	100g	24	5.6	0.5	0.1
Galia, without skin or seeds	1 slice [150g]	36	8.4	0.8	0.2
Honeydew, without skin or seeds	100g	28	6.6	0.6	0.1
Honeydew, without skin or seeds	1 slice [180g]	50	11.8	1.1	0.2

SPECIFIC	AMOUNT	KCALS	CARB	PROT	FAT
Watermelon, without skin or seeds	100g	31	7.1	0.5	0.3
Watermelon, without skin or seeds	1 slice [200g]	62	14.2	1.0	0.6
Mixed fruit					
dried	100g	268	68.1	2.3	0.4
dried	1 heaped tbsp [25g]	67	17.0	0.6	0.1
Nectarines					
raw, without stones	100g	40	9.0	1.4	0.1
raw, without stone	1 small [125g]	50	11.3	1.8	0.1
raw, without stone	1 medium [140g]	56	12.6	2.0	0.1
raw, without stone	1 large [175g]	70	15.8	3.5	0.2
Olives					
in brine	100g	103	trace	0.9	11.0
in brine	1 [3g]	3	trace	trace	0.3
Oranges					
raw, without skin	100g	37	8.5	1.1	0.1
raw, without skin	1 small [120g]	46	10.6	1.4	0.1
raw, without skin	1 medium [160g]	59	13.6	2.2	0.2
raw, without skin	1 large [210g]	78	17.9	2.3	2.2

SPECIFIC	AMOUNT	KCALS	CARB	PROT	FAT
Passion fruit					
raw, without skin	100g	36	5.8	2.6	0.4
raw, without skin	1 [15g]	5	0.9	0.4	trace
Paw-paw					
raw	100g	36	8.8	0.5	0.1
Peaches					
canned in juice	100g	39	9.7	0.6	trace
canned in juice	1 portion [105g]	41	10.2	0.6	trace
canned in syrup	100g	55	14.0	0.5	trace
canned in syrup	1 portion [105g]	58	14.7	0.5	trace
raw, without stone	100g	33	7.6	1.0	0.1
raw, without stone	1 small [70g]	23	5.3	0.7	trace
raw, without stone	1 medium [110g]	36	8.4	1.1	0.1
raw, without stone	1 large [150g]	50	11.4	1.5	0.2
Pears					
canned in juice	100g	33	8.5	0.3	trace
canned in juice	1 portion [120g]	40	10.2	0.4	trace
canned in syrup	100g	50	13.2	0.2	trace
canned in syrup	1 portion [120g]	60	15.8	0.2	trace
raw, without core	100g	40	10.0	0.3	0.1

SPECIFIC	AMOUNT	KCALS	CARB	PROT	FAT
raw, without core	1 medium [200g]	80	20.0	0.6	0.2
raw, peeled	100g	41	10.4	0.3	0.1
Peel					
mixed, dried	100g	231	59.1	0.3	0.9
Pineapple					
canned in juice	100g	47	12.2	0.3	trace
canned in juice	1 portion [120g]	56	14.6	0.3	trace
canned in syrup	100g	64	16.5	0.5	trace
canned in syrup	1 portion [120g]	77	20	0.6	trace
raw, without skin	100g	41	10.1	0.4	0.2
raw, without skin	1 slice [80g]	33	8.1	0.3	0.2
Plums					
canned in syrup	100g	59	15.5	0.3	trace
canned in syrup	1 portion [105g]	62	16.3	0.3	trace
raw, without stone	100g	34	8.3	0.5	0.1
raw, without stone	1 small [30g]	10	2.5	0.2	trace
raw, without stone	1 medium [55g]	19	4.6	0.3	0.1
raw, without stone	1 large [85g]	29	7.1	0.4	0.1
stewed with sugar, weighed with stones	100g	75	19.2	0.5	0.1

SPECIFIC	AMOUNT	KCALS	CARB	PROT	FAT
stewed with sugar, weighed with stones	1 portion [140g]	105	26.9	0.7	0.1
stewed without sugar, weighed with stones	100g	29	6.9	0.4	0.1
stewed without sugar, weighed without stones	1 portion [140g]	41	9.7	0.6	0.1
Prunes					
canned in juice	100g	79	19.7	0.7	0.2
canned in juice	1 portion [105g]	83	20.7	0.7	0.2
canned in syrup	100g	90	23.0	0.6	0.2
canned in syrup	1 portion [105g]	95	24.2	0.6	0.2
semi-dried, ready-to-eat	100g	141	34.0	2.5	0.4
semi-dried, ready-to-eat	1 [15g]	21	5.1	0.4	trace
Raisins					
	100g	272	69.3	2.1	0.4
	1 tbsp [30g]	82	20.8	0.6	trace
Raspberries					
canned in syrup	100g	31	7.6	0.5	trace
canned in syrup	1 portion [105g]	33	8.0	0.5	trace
raw	100g	25	4.6	1.4	0.3
raw	1 portion [60g]	15	2.8	0.8	0.2

SPECIFIC	AMOUNT	KCALS	CARB	PROT	FAT
Rhubarb					
canned in syrup	100g	65	16.9	0.5	trace
canned in syrup	1 portion [140g]	91	23.7	0.7	trace
raw	100g	7	0.8	0.9	0.1
stewed with sugar	100g	48	11.5	0.9	0.1
stewed with sugar	1 portion [140g]	67	16.1	1.3	0.1
stewed without sugar	100g	7	0.7	0.9	0.1
stewed without sugar	1 portion [140g]	10	1.0	1.3	0.1
Satsumas					
raw, without peel	100g	36	8.5	0.9	0.1
raw, without peel	1 small [50g]	18	4.3	0.5	0.1
raw, without peel	1 medium [70g]	25	6.0	0.6	0.1
raw, without peel	1 large [90g]	32	7.7	0.8	0.1
Strawberries					
canned in syrup	100g	65	16.9	0.5	trace
canned in syrup	1 portion [105g]	68	17.9	0.5	trace
raw	100g	27	6.0	0.8	0.1
raw	1 [12g]	3	6.1	0.1	trace
Sultanas	100g	275	69.4	2.7	0.4
	1 tbsp [30g]	83	20.8	0.8	trace

SPECIFIC	AMOUNT	KCALS	CARB	PROT	FAT
Tangerines					
raw	100g	35	8.0	0.9	0.1
raw	1 small [50g]	18	4.0	0.5	0.1
raw	1 medium [70g]	25	5.6	0.6	0.1
raw	1 large [90g]	32	7.2	0.6	0.1

VEGETABLES

SPECIFIC	AMOUNT	KCALS	CARB	PROT	FAT
Asparagus					
boiled	100 g	26	1.4	3.4	0.8
boiled	1 portion [125g/approx 5 spears]	33	1.7	4.3	1.0
raw	100g	25	2.0	2.9	0.6
Aubergine					
fried in corn oil	100g	302	2.8	1.2	31.9
fried in corn oil	1 portion [130g]	393	3.6	1.6	41.5
raw	100g	15	2.2	0.9	0.4
Bamboo Shoots					
canned, drained	100g	39	9.7	0.7	0
canned, drained	225g can	45	12.0	0.8	0
Beans					
Aduki, dried, boiled	100g	123	22.5	9.3	0.2
Aduki, dried, boiled	1 tbsp [30g]	37	6.8	2.8	trace
Baked, canned in tomato sauce	100g	84	15.3	5.2	0.6
Baked, canned in tomato sauce	1 small portion [80g]	67	12.2	4.2	0.5

Specific	Amount	Kcals	Carb	Prot	Fat
Baked, canned in tomato sauce	1 medium portion [135g]	113	20.7	7.0	0.8
Baked, canned in tomato sauce	1 large portion [190g]	160	29.1	9.9	1.1
Baked, canned in tomato sauce,	1 tbsp [45g]	38	6.9	2.3	0.3
Baked, canned in tomato sauce, reduced sugar	100g	73	12.5	5.4	0.6
Baked, canned in tomato sauce, reduced sugar	1 small portion [80g]	58	10.0	4.3	0.5
Baked, canned in tomato sauce, reduced sugar	1 medium portio [135g]	99	16.9	7.3	0.8
Baked, canned in tomato sauce, reduced sugar	1 large portion [190g]	139	23.8	10.3	1.1
Baked, canned in tomato sauce, reduced sugar	1 tbsp [45g]	33	5.6	2.4	0.3
Blackeye, dried, boiled	100g	116	19.9	8.8	0.7
Blackeye, dried, boiled	1 tbsp				
Broad, frozen, boiled	100g	81	11.7	7.9	0.6
Broad, frozen, boiled	1 portion [120g]	96	14.0	9.5	0.7
Butter, canned, re-heated, drained	100g	77	13.0	5.9	0.5
Butter, canned, re-heated, drained	1 portion [120g]	92	15.6	7.1	0.6
French, frozen, boiled	100g	25	4.7	1.7	0.1
French, frozen, boiled	1 small portion [60g]	15	2.8	1.0	0.1
French, frozen, boiled	1 medium portion [90g]	23	4.2	1.5	0.1

Specific	Amount	Kcals	Carb	Prot	Fat
French, frozen, boiled	1 large portion [120g]	30	5.6	2.0	0.1
French, raw	100g	24	3.2	1.9	0.5
Mung, dried, boiled	100g	91	15.3	7.6	0.4
Mung, dried, boiled	1 tbsp [30g]	27	4.6	2.3	0.1
Red kidney, canned, re-heated, drained	100g	100	17.8	6.9	0.6
Red kidney, canned, re-heated	1 portion [120g]	120	21.4	8.3	0.7
Red kidney, dried, boiled	100g	103	17.4	8.4	0.5
Red kidney, dried, boiled	1 tbsp [30g]	31	5.2	2.5	0.2
Runner, boiled	100g	186	2.3	1.2	0.5
Runner, boiled	1 small portion [60g]	11	1.4	0.7	0.2
Runner, boiled	1 medium portion [90g]	16	2.1	1.1	0.5
Runner, boiled	1 large portion [120g]	22	2.8	1.4	0.6
Runner, raw	100g	22	3.2	1.6	0.4
Soya, dried, boiled	100g	141	5.1	14.0	7.3
Soya, dried, boiled	1 tbsp [30g]	42	1.5	4.2	2.2
Beansprouts					
Mung, stir-fried in blended oil	100g	72	2.5	1.9	6.1
Mung, stir-fried in blended oil	1 portion [90g]	65	2.3	1.7	5.5
Mung, raw	100g	31	4.0	2.9	0.5

Specific	Amount	Kcals	Carb	Prot	Fat
Beetroot					
boiled	100g	46	9.5	2.3	0.1
boiled	1 slice [10g]	5	1.0	0.2	trace
pickled, drained	100g	28	5.6	1.2	0.2
pickled, drained	1 slice [10g]	3	0.6	0.1	trace
raw	100g	36	7.6	1.7	0.1
Black gram					
dried, boiled	100g	89	13.6	7.8	0.4
Broccoli					
boiled	100g	24	1.1	3.1	0.8
boiled	1 portion [90g]	22	1.0	2.8	0.7
raw	100g	33	1.8	4.4	0.9
Brussels sprouts					
boiled	100g	35	3.5	2.9	1.3
boiled	1 small portion [60g]	21	2.1	1.7	0.8
boiled	1 medium portion [90g]	32	3.2	2.6	1.2
boiled	1 large portion [120g]	42	4.2	3.5	1.6
frozen, boiled	100g	35	2.5	3.5	1.3
frozen, boiled	1 small portion [60g]	21	1.5	2.1	0.8
frozen, boiled	1 medium portion [90g]	32	2.3	3.2	1.2

SPECIFIC	AMOUNT	KCALS	CARB	PROT	FAT
frozen, boiled	1 large portion [120g]	42	3.0	4.2	1.6
raw	100g	42	4.1	5.3	1.4
Cabbage					
boiled	100g	18	2.5	0.8	0.6
boiled	1 small portion [60g]	11	1.5	0.5	0.4
boiled	1 medium portion [90g]	16	2.3	0.7	0.4
boiled	1 large portion [120g]	22	3.0	1.0	0.4
raw	100g	26	4.1	1.7	0.4
raw	1 medium portion [90g]	23	3.7	1.5	0.4
white, raw	100g	27	5.0	1.4	0.2
white, raw	1 medium portion [90g]	24	4.5	1.3	0.2
Carrots					
canned, re-heated, drained	100g	20	4.2	0.5	0.3
canned, re-heated, drained	3 medium carrots [36g]	7	1.5	0.2	0.1
old, boiled	100g	24	4.9	0.6	0.4
old, boiled	1 small portion [40g]	10	2.9	0.4	0.2
old, boiled	1 medium portion [60g]	14	1.2	0.2	0.1
old, boiled	1 large portion [85g]	20	1.7	0.2	0.1
old, raw	100g	35	2.5	0.3	0.2
old, raw	1 medium portion [60g]	21	1.5	0.2	0.1
young, boiled	100g	22	4.4	0.6	0.4

SPECIFIC	AMOUNT	KCALS	CARB	PROT	FAT
young, boiled	1 medium portion [60g]	13	2.6	0.4	0.2
young, raw	100g	30	6.0	0.7	0.5
young, raw	1 medium portion [60g]	18	3.6	0.4	0.3
Cauliflower					
boiled	100g	28	2.1	2.9	0.9
boiled	1 small portion [60g]	170	1.3	1.7	0.5
boiled	1 medium portion [90g]	25	1.9	2.6	0.8
boiled	1 large portion [120g]	34	2.5	3.5	1.1
raw	100g	34	3.0	3.6	0.9
raw	1 floret [10g]	3	0.3	0.4	trace
Celery					
boiled	100g	8	0.8	0.5	0.3
boiled	1 small portion [30g]	2	0.2	0.2	0.1
boiled	1 medium portion [50g]	4	0.4	0.3	0.2
boiled	1 large portion [85g]	7	0.7	0.4	0.3
raw	100g	7	0.9	0.5	0.2
raw	1 stick [30g]	2	0.3	0.2	0.1
Chick peas					
canned, re-heated, drained	100g	115	16.1	7.2	2.9
canned, re-heated, drained	1 medium portion [90g]	104	14.5	6.5	2.6

122

SPECIFIC	AMOUNT	KCALS	CARB	PROT	FAT
dried, boiled	100g	121	18.2	8.4	2.1
dried, boiled	1 heaped tbsp [28g]	34	5.1	2.4	0.6
Chicory					
raw	100g	11	2.8	0.5	0.6
Courgette					
boiled	100g	19	2.0	2.0	0.4
boiled	1 small portion [60g]	11	1.2	1.2	0.2
boiled	1 medium portion [90g]	17	1.8	1.8	0.2
boiled	1 large portion [120g]	23	2.4	2.4	0.2
fried in corn oil	100g	63	2.6	2.6	4.8
fried in corn oil	1 small portion [60g]	38	1.6	1.6	2.9
fried in corn oil	1 medium portion [90g]	57	2.3	2.3	4.3
fried in corn oil	1 large portion [120g]	76	3.1	3.1	5.8
raw	100g	18	1.8	1.8	0.4
Cucumber					
raw	100g	10	1.5	0.7	0.1
raw	1 inch piece [60g]	6	0.9	0.4	0.1
Curly Kale					
boiled	100g	24	1.0	2.4	1.1

123

Specific	Amount	Kcals	Carb	Prot	Fat
boiled	1 medium portion [90g]	14	0.6	1.4	0.7
raw	100g	33	1.4	3.4	1.6
Fennel					
boiled	100g	11	1.5	0.9	0.2
boiled	1 medium portion [50g]	6	0.8	0.5	0.1
raw	100g	12	1.8	0.9	0.2
Garlic					
raw	100g	98	16.3	7.9	0.6
Gherkins					
pickled, drained	100g	14	2.6	0.9	0.1
Gourd					
raw	100g	11	0.8	1.6	0.2
Hummus					
	100g	187	11.6	7.6	12.6
	1 tbsp [50g]	94	5.8	3.8	6.3
Leeks					
boiled	100g	21	2.6	1.2	0.7
boiled	1, average size [160g]	34	4.2	1.9	1.1

SPECIFIC	AMOUNT	KCALS	CARB	PROT	FAT
raw	100g	22	2.9	1.6	0.5
Lentils					
green and brown, whole, dried, boiled	100g	105	16.9	8.8	0.7
green and brown, whole, dried, boiled	1 tbsp [30g]	32	5.1	2.6	0.2
red, split, dried, boiled	100g	100	17.5	7.6	0.4
red, split, dried, boiled	1 tbsp [30g]	30	5.3	2.3	0.1
Lettuce					
average, raw	100g	14	1.7	0.8	0.5
average, raw	1 salad-size serving [30g]	4	0.5	0.2	0.2
Iceberg, raw	100g	13	1.9	0.7	0.3
Iceberg, raw	1 salad-size serving [80g]	10	0.6	0.2	0.1
Marrow					
boiled	100g	9	1.6	0.4	0.2
raw	100g	12	2.2	0.5	0.2
Mixed vegetables					
frozen, boiled	100g	42	6.6	3.3	0.5
frozen, boiled	1 medium serving [90g]	38	5.9	3.0	0.5

Specific	Amount	Kcals	Carb	Prot	Fat
with chilli, canned	100g	86	9.1	4.3	3.8
with chilli, canned	400g can	345	36.0	17.0	15.0
Mushrooms					
boiled	100g	11	0.4	1.8	0.3
creamed, canned	100g	80	5.4	3.4	5.0
creamed, canned	210g can	168	11.3	7.1	10.5
fried in blended oil	100g	157	0.3	2.4	16.2
fried in butter	100g	157	0.3	2.4	16.2
fried in corn oil	100g	157	0.3	2.4	16.2
fried	1 medium portion [45g]	71	0.1	1.1	7.3
raw	100g	13	0.4	1.8	0.5
raw	1, average [10g]	1	trace	0.2	trace
Mustard and Cress					
raw	100g	13	0.4	1.6	0.6
raw	1 tbsp [5g]	1	trace	0.1	trace
raw	1 punnet [40g]	5	0.2	0.6	0.2
Okra					
boiled	100g	28	2.7	2.5	0.9
raw	100g	31	3.0	2.8	1.0
raw	10, medium [50g]	16	1.5	1.4	0.5

126

Specific	Amount	Kcals	Carb	Prot	Fat
stir-fried in corn oil	100g	269	4.4	4.3	26.1
stir-fried in corn oil	1 medium portion [60g]	161	2.6	2.6	15.7
Onions					
boiled	100g	17	3.7	0.6	0.1
boiled	1 medium portion [60g]	10	2.2	0.4	0.1
cocktail/ silverskin, drained	100g	15	3.1	0.6	0.1
fried in blended oil	100g	164	14.1	2.3	11.2
fried in corn oil	100g	164	14.1	2.3	11.2
fried in lard	100g	164	14.1	2.3	11.2
fried	1 medium portion [57g]	98	8.5	1.4	6.7
pickled, drained	100g	24	4.9	0.9	0.2
pickled, drained	1, average [10g]	2	0.5	0.1	trace
pickled, drained	1, large [25g]	6	1.2	0.2	trace
raw	100g	36	7.9	1.2	0.2
raw	1, average [90g]	32	7.1	1.1	0.2
raw	1 slice [20g]	7	1.6	0.2	trace
Parsnip					
boiled	100g	66	12.9	1.6	1.2
boiled	1 small portion [40g]	26	5.2	0.6	0.5
boiled	1 medium portion [65g]	43	8.4	1.0	0.7
boiled	1 large portion [85g]	56	11.0	1.4	1.0

127

SPECIFIC	AMOUNT	KCALS	CARB	PROT	FAT
raw	100g	64	12.5	1.8	1.1
Peas					
boiled	100g	79	10.0	6.7	1.6
boiled	1 small portion [40g]	32	4	2.7	0.6
boiled	1 medium portion [65g]	51	6.5	4.4	1.0
boiled	1 large portion [85g]	67	8.5	5.7	1.4
canned, re-heated, drained	100g	80	13.5	5.3	0.9
canned, re-heated, drained	1 tbsp [30g]	24	4.1	1.6	0.3
frozen, boiled	100g	69	9.7	6.0	0.9
frozen, boiled	1 medium portion [65g]	45	6.3	3.9	0.6
Mange-tout, boiled	100g	261	3.3	3.2	0.1
Mange-tout, boiled	1 medium portion [50g]	13	1.7	1.6	0.1
Mange-tout, raw	100g	32	4.2	3.6	0.2
Mange-tout, stir-fried in blended oil	100g	71	3.5	3.8	4.8
mushy, canned, re-heated, drained	100g	81	13.8	5.8	0.7
mushy, canned, re-heated, drained	1 tbsp [30g]	24	4.1	1.7	0.2
Petits pois, frozen, boiled	100g	49	5.5	5.0	0.9
Petits pois, frozen, boiled	1 medium portion [65g]	32	3.6	3.3	0.6
processed, canned, re-heated, drained	100g	99	17.5	6.9	0.7
processed, canned, re-heated, drained	1 tbsp [30g]	30	5.3	2.1	0.2

SPECIFIC	AMOUNT	KCALS	CARB	PROT	FAT
raw	100g	83	11.3	6.9	1.5
Peppers					
Capsicum, green, boiled	100g	18	2.6	1.0	0.5
Capsicum, green, raw	100g	15	2.6	0.8	0.3
Capsicum, green, raw	1, medium [160g]	24	4.2	1.3	0.5
Capsicum, green, raw	1 sliced ring [10g]	2	0.3	0.1	trace
Capsicum, red, boiled	100g	34	7.0	1.1	0.4
Capsicum, red, raw	100g	32	6.4	1.0	0.4
Capsicum, red, raw	1, medium [160g]	51	10.2	1.6	0.6
Capsicum, red, raw	1 sliced ring [10g]	3	0.6	0.1	trace
mixed, raw	100g	20	0.7	2.9	0.6
Plantain					
boiled	100g	112	28.5	0.8	0.2
boiled	1, whole [200g]	224	57.0	1.6	0.4
fried in vegetable oil	100g	267	47.5	1.5	9.2
raw	100g	117	29.4	1.1	0.3
Potato croquettes					
fried in blended oil	100g	214	21.6	3.7	13.1
fried in blended oil	1, average [80g]	171	17.3	3.0	0.9

SPECIFIC	AMOUNT	KCALS	CARB	PROT	FAT
Potato powder					
instant, made up with water	100g	57	13.5	1.5	0.1
instant, made up with water	1 medium portion [180g]	103	24.3	2.7	0.18
instant, made up with whole milk	100g	76	14.8	2.4	1.2
instant, made up with whole milk	1 medium portion [180g]	137	26.7	4.3	2.2
Potato waffles					
frozen, cooked	100g	842	30.3	3.2	8.2
Potatoes (Chips)					
fine cut, frozen, fried in blended oil	100g	364	41.2	4.5	21.3
fine cut, frozen, fried in corn oil	100g	364	41.2	4.5	21.3
fine cut, frozen, fried in dripping	100g	364	41.2	4.5	21.3
fine cut, frozen, fried	1 small portion [130g]	473	53.6	5.9	27.7
fine cut, fried	1 medium portion [180g]	655	74.2	8.1	38.3
fine cut, fried	1 large portion [240g]	874	98.9	10.8	51.12
homemade, fried in blended oil	100g	189	30.1	3.9	6.7
homemade, fried in corn oil	100g	189	30.1	3.9	6.7
homemade, fried in dripping	100g	189	30.1	3.9	6.7

SPECIFIC	AMOUNT	KCALS	CARB	PROT	FAT
homemade, fried	1 small portion [130g]	246	39.1	5.1	8.7
homemade, fried	1 medium portion [180g]	340	54.2	7.0	12.1
homemade, fried	1 large portion [240g]	454	72.2	9.4	20.1
oven, frozen, baked	100g	162	29.8	3.2	4.2
oven, frozen, baked	1 medium portion [180g]	292	53.6	5.8	7.6
chip shop, fried in dripping	100g	239	30.5	3.2	12.4
chip shop, fried in blended oil	100g	239	30.5	3.2	12.4
chip shop, fried in vegetable oil	100g	239	30.5	3.2	12.4
chip shop, fried	1 average serving [200g]	478	61.0	6.4	24.8
straight cut, frozen, fried in blended oil	100g	273	36.0	4.1	13.5
straight cut, frozen, fried in corn oil	100g	273	36.0	4.1	13.5
straight cut, frozen, fried in dripping	100g	273	36.0	4.1	13.5
straight cut, frozen, fried	1 portion [180g]	491	64.8	7.4	24
french fries, retail [burger restaurants]	100g	280	34.0	3.3	15.5
french fries, retail [burger restaurants]	1 regular serving [105g]	294	35.7	3.5	16.3
french fries, retail [burger restaurants]	1 regular serving [150g]	420	51	5.0	23.3

131

SPECIFIC	AMOUNT	KCALS	CARB	PROT	FAT
Potatoes (New)					
boiled	100g	75	17.8	1.5	0.3
boiled	1 small portion [120g]	90	21.4	1.8	0.4
boiled	1 medium portion [180g]	135	32.0	2.7	0.5
boiled	1 large portion [220g]	165	39.2	3.3	0.7
boiled in skins	100g	66	15.4	1.4	0.3
boiled in skins	1 small portion [120g]	79	18.5	1.7	0.4
boiled in skins	1 medium portion [180g]	119	27.7	2.5	0.5
boiled in skins	1 large portion [220g]	145	33.9	3.1	0.7
canned, re-heated, drained	100g	63	15.1	1.5	0.1
canned, re-heated	1 medium portion [180g]	113	27.2	2.7	0.2
raw	100g	70	16.1	1.7	0.3
Potatoes (Old)					
baked, flesh and skin	100g	136	31.7	3.9	0.2
baked, flesh and skin	1 medium-size [180g]	245	57.1	7.0	0.4
baked, flesh only	100g	77	18.0	2.2	0.1
baked, flesh only	1 medium-size [160g]	123	28.8	3.5	0.2

SPECIFIC	AMOUNT	KCALS	CARB	PROT	FAT
boiled	100g	72	17.0	1.8	0.1
boiled	1 small portion [120g]	86	20.4	2.2	0.1
boiled	1 medium portion [180g]	130	30.6	3.2	0.2
boiled	1 large portion [220g]	158	37.4	4.0	0.2
boiled, mashed with butter	100g	104	15.5	1.8	4.3
boiled, mashed with margarine	100g	104	15.5	1.8	4.3
boiled, mashed with butter or margarine	1 medium portion [180g]	187	27.9	3.2	7.7
raw	100g	75	17.2	2.1	0.2
roast in blended oil	100g	149	25.9	2.9	4.5
roast in corn oil	100g	149	25.9	2.9	4.5
roast in lard	100g	149	25.9	2.9	4.5
roast	1 medium portion [200g]	298	51.8	5.8	9.0
Pumpkin					
raw	100g	13	2.2	0.7	0.2
boiled	100g	13	2.1	0.6	0.3
Quorn	100g	86	2.0	11.8	3.5

SPECIFIC	AMOUNT	KCALS	CARB	PROT	FAT
Radish					
raw	100g	12	1.9	0.7	0.2
raw	1, average [10g]	1	0.2	0.1	trace
Ratatouille					
canned	100g	38	3.0	1.0	2.5
canned	400g can	150	12.0	4.0	10.0
Spinach					
boiled	100g	19	0.8	2.2	0.8
boiled	1 medium portion [90g]	17	0.7	2.0	0.7
frozen, boiled	100g	21	0.5	3.1	0.8
frozen, boiled	1 medium portion [90g]	19	0.5	2.8	0.7
raw	100g	25	1.6	2.8	0.8
Spring greens					
boiled	100g	20	1.6	1.9	0.7
boiled	1 medium portion [90g]	18	1.4	1.7	0.6
raw	100g	33	3.1	3.0	1.0
Spring onions					
raw	100g	23	3.0	2.0	0.5

134

Specific	Amount	Kcals	Carb	Prot	Fat
raw	1, average [20g]	5	0.6	0.4	0.1
Swede					
raw	100g	24	5.0	0.7	0.3
boiled	100g	11	2.3	0.3	0.1
boiled	1 small portion [40g]	4	0.9	0.1	trace
boiled	1 medium portion [60g]	7	1.4	0.1	0.1
boiled	1 large portion [85g]	9	2.0	0.3	0.1
Sweet potato					
boiled	100g	84	20.5	1.1	0.3
boiled	2, medium [130g]	109	26.7	1.4	0.4
raw	100g	87	21.3	1.2	0.3
Sweetcorn					
baby, canned, drained	100g	23	2.0	2.9	0.4
kernels, canned, drained	100g	122	26.6	2.9	1.2
kernels, canned, drained	1 tbsp [30g]	37	8.0	0.9	0.4
on-the-cob, whole, boiled	100g	66	11.6	2.5	1.4
on-the-cob, whole, boiled	1, kernels only [125g]	83	14.5	3.1	1.8
Tofu					
Soya bean, steamed	100g	73	0.7	8.1	4.2

SPECIFIC	AMOUNT	KCALS	CARB	PROT	FAT
Soya bean, steamed, fried	100g	261	2.0	23.5	17.7
Tomato-based product					
Passata	100g	29	6.0	1.1	0.2
Passata	550g jar	160	33.0	6.1	1.1
Tomato puree	100g	68	12.9	4.5	0.2
Tomatoes					
canned, with juice	100g	16	3.0	1.0	0.1
fried in blended oil	100g	91	5.0	0.7	7.7
fried in corn oil	100g	91	5.0	0.7	7.7
fried in lard	100g	91	5.0	0.7	7.7
grilled	100g	49	8.9	2.0	0.9
raw	100g	17	3.1	0.7	0.3
raw	1, small [65g]	117	2.0	0.5	0.2
raw	1, medium [85g]	14	2.6	0.6	0.3
raw	1, large [150g]	26	4.7	0.8	0.3
Turnip					
boiled	100g	12	2.0	0.6	0.2
boiled	1 small portion [40g]	5	0.8	0.2	0.1
boiled	1 medium portion [60g]	7	1.2	0.4	0.1
boiled	1 large portion [85g]	10	1.7	0.5	0.2

Specific	Amount	Kcals	Carb	Prot	Fat
raw	100g	23	4.7	0.9	0.3
Watercress					
raw	100g	22	0.4	3.0	1.0
raw	1 bunch [80g]	18	0.3	2.4	0.8
Yam					
boiled	100g	133	33.0	1.7	0.3
boiled	1, medium [130g]	173	42.9	2.2	0.4
raw	100g	114	28.2	1.5	0.3

137

NUTS AND SEEDS

SPECIFIC	AMOUNT	KCALS	CARB	PROT	FAT
Nuts					
Almonds	100g	612	6.9	21.1	55.8
	6 whole [10g]	61	0.7	2.1	5.6
Brazil nuts	100g	682	3.1	14.1	68.2
	6 whole [20g]	136	0.6	2.8	13.6
Cashew nuts					
roasted, salted	100g	611	18.8	20.5	50.9
roasted, salted	10 whole [10g]	61	1.9	2.1	5.1
roasted, salted	25g packet	153	4.7	5.1	12.7
Chestnuts	100g	170	36.6	2.0	2.7
	5 whole [50g]	85	18.3	1.0	1.4
Coconut					
creamed, block	100g	669	7.0	6.0	68.8
dessicated	100g	604	6.4	5.6	62.0

SPECIFIC	AMOUNT	KCALS	CARB	PROT	FAT
Hazelnuts	100g	650	6.0	14.1	63.5
	10 whole [10g]	65	0.6	1.4	6.4
Macademia nuts					
salted	100g	748	4.8	7.9	77.6
salted	6 nuts [10g]	75	0.5	0.8	7.8
Mixed nuts	100g	607	7.9	22.9	54.1
	40g packet	243	3.2	9.2	21.6
	50g packet	304	4.0	11.5	27.1
Peanuts					
plain	100g	564	12.5	25.6	46.1
plain	10 whole [10g]	56	1.3	2.6	4.6
roasted, salted	100g	602	7.1	24.5	53.0
roasted, salted	10 whole [10g]	60	0.7	2.5	5.3
roasted, salted	25g packet	151	1.8	6.1	13.3
roasted, salted	40g packet	241	2.8	9.8	21
roasted, salted	50g packet	301	3.6	12.3	26.5
dry roasted	100g	589	10.3	25.5	49.8
dry roasted	40g packet	236	4.1	10.2	19.9
Pecan nuts	100g	689	5.8	9.2	70.1

SPECIFIC	AMOUNT	KCALS	CARB	PROT	FAT
	3 nuts [18g]	124	1.0	1.7	12.6
Pine nuts	100g	688	4.0	14.0	68.6
Pistachio nuts	100g	331	4.6	9.9	30.5
	10 nuts [8g]	26	0.4	0.8	2.4
Walnuts	100g	688	3.3	14.7	68.5
	6 halves [20g]	138	0.7	2.9	13.7
Nut-based products					
Marzipan, home-made	100g	461	50.2	10.4	25.8
Marzipan, retail	100g	404	67.6	5.3	14.4
Peanut butter, smooth	100g	623	13.1	22.6	53.7
Peanut butter, smooth	generous spreading for bread [20g]	125	2.6	4.5	10.7
Peanut butter, smooth	thin spreading for bread [12g]	75	1.6	2.7	6.4
Seeds					
Sesame seeds	100g	578	0.9	18.2	58.0
	1 tbsp [10g]	58	0.1	1.8	5.8
Sunflower seeds	100g	581	18.6	19.8	47.5

SPECIFIC	AMOUNT	KCALS	CARB	PROT	FAT
	1 tbsp [14g]	81	2.6	2.8	6.7
Seed-based products					
Tahini [sesame seed spread]	100g	607	0.9	18.5	58.9
Tahini [sesame seed spread]	1 heaped tsp [19g]	115	0.2	3.5	11.2

CEREALS AND CEREAL PRODUCTS

Specific	Amount	Kcals	Carb	Prot	Fat
Biscuits					
Cheddars, mini	100g	534	52.9	11.3	30.2
Cheeselets	100g	464	56.9	10.3	21.7
Cheeselets	1 biscuit	5	0.6	0.1	3.3
Chocolate, assorted	100g	524	67.4	5.7	27.6
Club, mint	100g	521	58.9	3.8	30.0
Club, mint	1 biscuit	133	15.1	1.0	7.7
Club, double choc	100g	539	59.3	5.1	29.8
Club, double choc	1 biscuit	127	14.0	1.2	7.0
Digestive	100g	499	67.0	6.5	22.1
Digestive	1 biscuit	73	9.8	1.0	3.3
Digestive with plain chocolate	100g	511	60.8	7.6	26.1
Digestive with plain chocolate	1 biscuit	85	10.0	1.3	4.4
Flapjacks	100g	484	60.4	4.5	26.6
Garibaldis	100g	409	70.5	4.0	9.4
Garibaldis	1 biscuit	45	7.3	0.4	1.0
Gingernut	100g	456	79.1	5.6	15.2
Hob nobs	100g	490	65.3	7.1	21.9
Hob nobs	1 biscuit	72	9.6	1.0	3.2
Homemade	100g	463	64.3	6.2	21.9

Specific	Amount	Kcals	Carb	Prot	Fat
Jaffa cakes	100g	363	67.8	3.5	10.5
Sandwich	100g	513	69.2	5.0	25.9
Semi-sweet	100g	457	74.8	6.7	16.6
Short-sweet	100g	469	62.2	6.2	23.4
Wafer, filled	100g	535	66.0	4.7	29.9
Oatcakes	100g	441	63.0	10.0	18.3
Shortbread	100g	498	63.9	5.9	26.1
Bran					
Wheat	100g	206	26.8	14.1	5.5
Wheat	1 tbsp [7g]	14	1.9	1.0	0.4
Bread					
Brown, average	100g	218	44.3	8.5	2.0
Brown, average	25g slice	54.5	1.8	2.0	0.5
Chapatis, made with fat	100g	328	48.3	8.1	12.8
Chapatis, made with fat	1 [60g]	197	29.0	4.9	7.7
Chapatis, made without fat	100g	202	43.7	7.3	1.0
Chapatis, made without fat	1 [55g]	111	24.0	4.0	0.6
Croissants	100g	360	38.3	8.3	20.3
Croissants	1, average, plain [50g]	180	19.2	4.2	10.2
Crumpets, toasted	100g	199	43.4	6.7	1.0
Crumpets, toasted	1 [40g]	80	17.4	2.7	0.4

SPECIFIC	AMOUNT	KCALS	CARB	PROT	FAT
Currant	100g	289	50.7	7.5	7.6
Currant	30g slice	87	15.2	2.3	2.3
Granary	100g	235	46.3	9.3	2.7
Granary	25g slice	59	11.6	2.3	0.7
Hovis	100g	212	41.5	9.5	2.0
Hovis	25g slice	53	10.4	2.4	0.5
Malt	100g	268	56.8	8.3	2.4
Malt	35g slice	93.8	19.9	2.9	0.8
Naan	100g	336	50.1	8.9	12.5
Naan	160g portion	538	80.2	14.2	20.0
Pitta	100g	265	57.9	9.2	1.2
Pitta	75g pitta	199	43.4	6.9	0.9
Pitta	95g pitta	252	55.0	8.7	1.1
Rolls, brown, crusty	100g	255	50.4	10.3	2.8
Rolls, brown, crusty	1 roll [48g]	122	22.7	4.9	1.3
Rolls, brown, soft	100g	268	51.8	10.0	2.8
Rolls, brown, soft	1 roll [43g]	115	22.3	4.3	1.2
Rolls, hamburger buns	100g	264	48.8	9.1	5.0
Rolls, hamburger buns	1 roll [50g]	132	24.4	4.6	2.5
Rolls, white, crusty	100g	280	57.6	10.9	2.3
Rolls, white, crusty	1 roll [50g]	140	28.8	5.5	1.2
Rolls, white, soft	100g	268	51.6	9.2	4.2
Rolls, white, soft	1 roll [45g]	121	23.2	4.4	1.9

SPECIFIC	AMOUNT	KCALS	CARB	PROT	FAT
Rolls, wholemeal	100g	241	48.3	9.0	2.9
Rolls, wholemeal	1 roll [45g]	108	21.7	4.1	1.3
Rye	100g	219	45.8	8.3	1.7
Rye	25g slice	55	11.5	2.1	0.4
Vitbe	100g	229	43.4	9.7	3.1
Vitbe	25g slice	57	10.9	2.4	0.8
White, 'with added fibre'	100g	230	49.6	7.6	1.5
White, 'with added fibre'	25g slice	58	12.4	1.9	0.4
White, average	100g	235	49.3	8.4	1.9
White, average	25g slice	59	12.3	2.1	0.5
White, french stick	100g	270	55.4	9.6	2.7
White, french stick	2 inch stick [40g]	108	22.2	3.8	1.1
White, fried	100g	503	48.5	7.9	32.2
White, fried	35g slice	176	17.0	2.8	11.3
White, sliced	100g	217	46.8	7.6	1.3
White, sliced	25g slice	54	11.7	1.9	0.3
Wholemeal, average	100g	215	41.6	9.2	2.5
Wholemeal, average	25g slice	54	10.4	2.3	0.6
Breakfast cereal					
All-bran	100g	261	46.6	14.0	3.4
All-bran	medium portion [50g]	131	23.3	7.0	1.7
Bran Flakes	100g	318	69.3	10.2	1.9

146

SPECIFIC	AMOUNT	KCALS	CARB	PROT	FAT
Bran Flakes	medium portion [40g]	127	27.7	4.1	0.8
Coco Pops	100g	384	74.0	5.3	1.0
Coco Pops	medium portion [30g]	115	22.2	1.6	0.3
Common Sense Oat Bran Flakes	100g	357	85.9	11.0	4.0
Common Sense Oat Bran Flakes	medium portion [40g]	143	34.4	4.4	1.6
Corn Flakes	100g	360	88.6	7.9	0.7
Corn Flakes	medium portion [40g]	144	35.4	3.2	0.3
Crunchy Nut Corn Flakes	100g	398	93.7	7.4	4.0
Crunchy Nut Corn Flakes	medium portion [40g]	159	37.5	3.0	1.6
Frosties	100g	377	93.7	5.3	0.5
Frosties	medium portion [40g]	151	37.5	2.1	0.2
Fruit'n Fibre	100g	349	72.1	9.0	4.7
Fruit'n Fibre	medium portion [40g]	140	28.8	3.6	1.9
Muesli	medium portion [80g]	290	57.8	7.8	4.7
Muesli with no added sugar	100g	366	67.1	10.5	7.8
Muesli with no added sugar	medium portion [80g]	293	53.7	8.4	6.2
Muesli, Swiss style	100g	363	72.2	9.8	5.9
Oat and Wheat Bran	100g	325	67.7	10.6	3.5
Oat and Wheat Bran	medium portion [40g]	130	27.1	4.2	1.4
Porridge, made with milk	medium portion [200g]	232	27.4	9.6	10.2
Porridge, made with water	medium portion [200g]	98	18.0	3.0	2.2

SPECIFIC	AMOUNT	KCALS	CARB	PROT	FAT
Porridge, with milk	100g	116	13.7	4.8	5.1
Porridge, with water	100g	49	9.0	1.5	1.1
Puffed Wheat	100g	321	67.3	14.2	1.3
Puffed Wheat	medium portion [40g]	128	26.9	5.7	0.5
Raisin Splitz	100g	337	75.4	9.0	2.0
Raisin Splitz	medium portion [40g]	135	30.2	3.6	0.8
Ready Brek	100g	373	68.6	11.4	7.8
Ready Brek	medium portion [180g]	671	123.5	20.5	14.0
Rice Krispies	100g	369	89.7	6.1	0.9
Rice Krispies	medium portion [30g]	111	26.9	1.8	0.3
Ricicles	100g	381	95.7	4.3	0.5
Ricicles	medium portion [30g]	114	28.7	1.3	0.2
Shredded Wheat	100g	325	68.3	10.6	3.0
Shredded Wheat	1 piece [22g]	72	304	15.0	2.3
Shreddies	100g	331	74.1	10.1	1.5
Shreddies	medium portion [50g]	166	37.1	5.1	0.8
Smacks	100g	386	89.6	8.0	2.0
Smacks	medium portion [40g]	154	35.8	3.2	0.8
Special K	100g	377	81.7	15.3	1.0
Special K	medium portion [30g]	113	24.5	4.6	0.3
Start	100g	355	81.7	7.9	1.7
Start	medium portion [40g]	142	32.7	3.2	0.7
Sugar Puffs	100g	348	84.5	5.9	0.8

148

SPECIFIC	AMOUNT	KCALS	CARB	PROT	FAT
Sugar Puffs	medium portion [40g]	139	33.8	2.4	0.3
Sultana Bran	100g	303	67.8	8.5	1.6
Sultana Bran	medium portion [50g]	121	33.9	4.3	0.8
Weetabix	100g	352	75.7	11.0	2.7
Weetabix	1 piece [20g]	70	15.1	2.2	0.5
Weetaflakes	100g	359	79.3	9.2	2.8
Weetaflakes	medium portion [40g]	144	31.7	3.7	1.1
Weetos	100g	372	86.1	6.1	2.7
Weetos	medium portion [40g]	149	34.4	2.4	1.1
Buns					
Chelsea	100g	366	56.1	7.8	13.8
Chelsea	1 bun [78g]	285	43.8	6.1	10.8
Currant	100g	296	52.7	7.6	7.5
Currant	1 bun [60g]	178	31.6	4.6	4.5
Hot cross	100g	310	58.5	7.4	6.8
Hot cross	1 bun [50g]	155	29.3	3.7	3.4
Cakes					
Battenburg	100g	370	50.0	5.9	17.5
Battenburg	40g slice	148	20	2.4	7.0
Chocolate Krispie, individual	100g	464	73.1	5.6	18.6
Chocolate Krispie, individual	1 cake [25g]	116	18.3	1.4	4.7

Specific	Amount	Kcals	Carb	Prot	Fat
Doughnuts, jam	100g	336	48.8	5.7	14.5
Doughnuts, jam	1 [75g]	252	3.4	4.3	10.9
Doughnuts, ring	100g	397	47.2	6.1	21.7
Doughnuts, ring	1 [60g]	238	28.3	3.7	13.0
Eclairs	100g	396	26.1	5.6	30.6
Eclairs	1 [90g]	356	23.5	5.0	27.5
Fancy Iced, individual	100g	407	68.8	3.8	14.9
Fancy Iced, individual	1 cake [30g]	122	20.6	1.1	4.5
Fruit, plain	100g	354	57.9	5.1	12.9
Fruit, plain	90g slice	319	52.1	4.6	11.6
Fruit, rich	100g	341	59.6	3.8	11.0
Fruit, rich	70g slice	239	41.7	2.7	7.7
Fruit, rich, iced	100g	356	62.7	4.1	11.4
Fruit, rich, iced	70g slice	249	43.9	2.9	8.0
Fruit, wholemeal	100g	363	52.8	6.0	15.7
Fruit, wholemeal	90g slice	327	47.5	5.4	14.1
Gateau	100g	337	43.4	5.7	16.8
Gateau	85g slice	286	36.9	4.8	14.3
Madeira	100g	393	58.4	5.4	16.9
Madeira	40g slice	157	23.4	2.2	6.8
Sponge, basic	100g	459	52.4	6.4	26.3
Sponge, basic	53g slice	243	22.5	2.8	11.3
Sponge, fatless	100g	294	53.0	10.1	6.1

SPECIFIC	AMOUNT	KCALS	CARB	PROT	FAT
Sponge, fatless	53g slice	156	28.1	5.4	3.2
Sponge, jam filled	100g	302	64.2	4.2	4.9
Sponge, jam, filled	65g slice	196	41.7	2.7	3.2
Sponge, butter icing	100g	490	52.4	4.5	30.6
Sponge, butter icing	65g slice	319	34.1	2.9	19.9
Swiss Rolls, chocolate, individual	100g	337	58.1	4.3	11.3
Swiss Rolls, chocolate, individual	1 roll [26g]	88	16.3	1.2	2.9
Teacakes	100g	329	58.3	8.9	8.3
Teacakes	1 [60g]	197	35.0	5.3	5.0
Crackers					
Cream	100g	440	68.3	9.5	16.3
Cream	1 [7g]	31	4.8	0.7	1.1
Wholemeal	100g	413	72.1	10.1	11.3
Wholemeal	1 [15g]	62	10.8	1.5	1.7
Crispbread					
Rye	100g	321	70.6	9.4	2.1
Rye	1 [10g]	32	7.1	0.9	0.2
Custard powder	100g	354	92.0	0.6	0.7

Specific	Amount	Kcals	Carb	Prot	Fat
Flour					
Chapati brown	100g	333	73.7	11.5	1.2
Chapati, brown	1 level tbsp [20g]	66.6	14.7	2.3	0.2
Chapati white	100g	335	77.6	9.8	0.5
Chapati, white	1 level tbsp [20g]	67	15.5	2.0	0.1
Cornflour	100g	354	92.0	0.6	0.7
Cornflour	1 level tbsp [20g]	71	18	0.1	0.1
Rye flour	100g	335	75.9	8.2	2.0
Rye flour	1 level tbsp [20g]	67	15.2	1.6	0.4
Soya , full fat	100g	447	23.5	36.8	23.5
Soya, full fat	1 level tbsp [20g]	89	4.7	7.4	4.7
Soya, low fat	100g	352	28.2	45.3	7.2
Soya, low fat	1 level tbsp [20g]	70	5.6	9.1	1.4
Wheat , brown	100g	323	68.5	12.6	1.8
Wheat, brown	1 level tbsp [20g]	65	13.7	2.5	0.4
Wheat, white, breadmaking	100g	341	75.3	11.5	1.4
Wheat, white, breadmaking	1 level tbsp [20g]	68	15.1	2.3	0.5
Wheat, white, plain	100g	341	77.7	9.4	1.3
Wheat, white, plain	1 level tbsp [20g]	68	15.5	1.9	0.3
Wheat, white, self-raising	100g	330	75.6	8.9	1.2
Wheat, white, self-raising	1 level tbsp [20g]	66	15.1	1.8	0.2
Wheat, wholemeal	100g	310	63.9	12.7	2.2
Wheat, wholemeal	1 level tbsp [20g]	62	12.8	2.5	0.4

SPECIFIC	AMOUNT	KCALS	CARB	PROT	FAT
Noodles					
Egg, raw	100g	391	71.7	12.1	8.2
Egg, boiled	100g	62	13.0	2.2	0.5
Egg, boiled	300g packet	186	39	6.6	1.5
Oatmeal					
raw	100g	375	66.0	11.2	9.2
Pancakes					
Scotch	100g	292	43.6	5.8	11.7
Scotch	1, [50g]	146	21.8	2.9	5.9
Pasta					
Macaroni, raw	100g	348	75.8	12.0	1.8
Macaroni, boiled	100g	86	18.5	3.0	0.5
Macaroni, boiled	medium portion [230g]	198	42.6	6.9	1.2
Spaghetti, white, raw	100g	342	74.1	12.0	1.8
Spaghetti, white, boiled	100g	104	22.2	3.6	0.7
Spaghetti, boiled	medium portion [230g]	239	51.1	8.3	1.6
Spaghetti, wholemeal, raw	100g	324	66.2	13.4	2.5
Spaghetti, wholemeal, boiled	100g	113	23.2	4.7	0.9
Spaghetti, wholemeal, boiled	medium portion [230g]	260	53.4	10.8	2.1

Specific	Amount	Kcals	Carb	Prot	Fat
Pastries					
Cream Horns	100g	435	25.8	3.8	35.8
Cream Horns	1 [60g]	261	15.5	2.3	21.5
Custard tarts, individual	100g	277	32.4	6.3	14.5
Custard tarts, individual	1 [94g]	260	30.5	5.9	13.6
Danish	100g	374	51.3	5.8	17.6
Danish	1, medium [110g]	411	56.4	6.4	19.4
Eccles cakes	100g	475	59.3	3.9	26.4
Eccles cakes	1 [45g]	214	26.7	1.8	11.9
Greek	100g	322	40.0	4.7	17.0
Jam tarts	100g	380	62.0	3.3	13.0
Jam tarts	90g slice	342	55.8	3.0	11.7
Mince pies, individual	100g	423	59.0	4.3	20.4
Mince pies, individual	1 [48g]	203	28.3	1.2	9.8
Flaky, raw	100g	424	34.8	4.2	30.7
Flaky, cooked	100g	560	45.9	5.6	40.6
Shortcrust, raw	100g	449	46.8	5.7	27.9
Shortcrust, cooked	100g	521	54.2	6.6	32.3
Wholemeal, raw	100g	431	38.5	7.7	28.4
Wholemeal, cooked	100g	499	44.6	8.9	32.9

154

SPECIFIC	AMOUNT	KCALS	CARB	PROT	FAT
Puddings					
Blackcurrant pie, pastry top and bottom	100g	262	34.5	3.1	13.3
Blackcurrant pie, pastry top and bottom	120g portion	314	41.4	3.7	16.0
Bread pudding	100g	297	49.7	5.9	9.6
Bread pudding	170g portion	505	84.5	10.0	16.3
Christmas pudding, home made	100g [average portion]	291	49.5	4.6	9.7
Christmas pudding, retail	100g [average portion]	329	56.3	3.0	11.8
Crumble, fruit	100g	198	34.0	2.0	6.9
Crumble, fruit	170g portion	337	57.8	3.4	11.7
Crumble, fruit, wholemeal	100g	193	31.7	2.6	7.1
Crumble, fruit, wholemeal	170g portion	328	53.9	4.4	12.1
Fruit pie, top crust only	100g	186	28.7	2.0	7.9
Fruit pie, top crust only	120g portion	223	34.4	2.4	9.4
Fruit pie, pastry top and bottom	100g	260	34.0	3.0	13.3
Fruit pie, pastry top and bottom	120g portion	312	40.8	3.6	16.0
Fruit pie, individual	100g	369	56.7	4.3	15.5
Fruit pie, individual	1 [50g]	185	28.4	2.2	7.8
Fruit pie, wholemeal, top crust only	100g	183	26.6	2.6	8.1
Fruit pie, wholemeal, top crust only	120g portion	220	31.9	3.1	9.7
Fruit pie, wholemeal, pastry top and bottom	100g	251	30.0	4.0	13.6

SPECIFIC	AMOUNT	KCALS	CARB	PROT	FAT
Fruit pie, wholemeal, pastry					
top and bottom	120g slice	301	36	4.8	16.3
Lemon meringue pie	100g	319	45.9	4.5	14.4
Lemon meringue pie	120g slice	383	55.1	5.4	17.3
Pancakes, sweet, made with whole milk	100g	301	35.0	5.9	16.2
Pancakes, sweet, made with whole milk	110g portion	331	38.5	6.5	17.8
Pie, with pie filling	100g	273	34.6	3.2	14.5
Pie, with pie filling	120g portion	328	41.5	3.8	17.4
Sponge pudding	100g	340	45.3	5.8	16.3
Sponge pudding	170g portion	578	77	9.8	27.7
Treacle tart	100g	368	60.4	3.7	14.1
Treacle tart	120g portion	322	72.5	4.4	16.9
Rice					
Brown, raw	100g	357	81.3	6.7	2.8
Brown, boiled	100g	141	32.1	2.6	1.1
Brown, boiled	medium portion [150g]	212	48.2	3.9	1.7
Savoury, raw	100g	415	77.4	8.4	10.3
Savoury, cooked	100g	142	26.3	2.9	3.5
Savoury, cooked	medium portion [150g]	213	39.5	4.4	5.3
White, easy cook, raw	100g	383	85.8	7.3	3.6
White, easy cook, boiled	100g	138	30.9	2.6	1.3
White, easy cook, boiled	medium portion [150g]	207	46.4	3.9	2.0

SPECIFIC	AMOUNT	KCALS	CARB	PROT	FAT
White, fried in lard	100g	131	25.0	2.2	3.2
White, fried in lard	300g portion	393	75.0	6.6	9.6
Sago					
raw	100g	355	94.0	0.2	0.2
Cauliflower cheese	100g	105	5.1	5.9	6.9
	200g portion as main dish	210	10.2	11.8	13.8
	90g portion as side dish	95	4.6	5.3	6.2
Savouries					
Dumplings	100g	208	24.5	2.8	11.7
Macaroni cheese	100g	178	13.6	7.3	10.8
Macaroni cheese	300g portion	534	40.8	21.9	32.4
Pancakes, savoury, made with whole milk	100g	273	24.0	6.3	17.5
Ravioli, canned in tomato sauce	100g	70	10.3	3.0	2.2
Ravioli, canned in tomato sauce	200g portion	140	20.6	6.0	4.4

SPECIFIC	AMOUNT	KCALS	CARB	PROT	FAT
Risotto, plain	100g	224	34.4	3.0	9.3
Risotto, plain	300g portion	672	103.2	9.0	27.9
Samosas, meat	100g	593	17.9	5.1	56.1
Samosas, vegetable	100g	472	22.3	3.1	41.8
Spaghetti, canned in tomato sauce	100g	64	14.1	1.9	0.4
Spaghetti, canned in tomato sauce	125g portion	80	17.6	2.4	0.5
Stuffing, sage and onion	100g	231	20.4	5.2	14.8
Stuffing mix	100g	338	67.2	9.9	5.2
Stuffing mix, made up with water	100g	97	19.3	2.8	1.5
Yorkshire pudding	100g	208	24.7	6.6	9.9
Scones					
Fruit	100g	316	52.9	7.3	9.8
Plain	100g	362	53.8	7.2	14.6
Wholemeal	100g	326	43.1	5.8	11.7
Tapioca					
raw	100g	359	95.0	0.4	0.1
Wheatgerm	100g	357	44.7	26.7	9.2

Egg and Egg-based Dishes

Specific	Amount	Kcals	Carb	Prot	Fat
Chicken's egg					
boiled	100g	147	trace	12.5	10.8
boiled	1, size 1 [67g]	98	trace	8.4	7.2
boiled	1, size 2 [61g]	90	trace	7.6	6.6
boiled	1, size 3 [57g]	84	trace	7.1	6.2
boiled	1, size 4 [47g]	69	trace	5.9	5.1
fried in vegetable oil	100g	179	trace	13.6	13.9
fried in vegetable oil	1, average [60g]	107	trace	8.2	8.3
poached	100g	147	trace	12.5	10.8
poached	1, average [50g]	74	trace	6.3	5.4
scrambled, with milk	100g	247	0.6	10.7	22.6
scrambled, with milk	2 eggs [120g]	296	0.7	12.8	27.1
white, raw	100g	36	trace	9.0	trace
whole, raw	100g	147	trace	12.5	10.8
whole, raw	1, size 1 [67g]	98	trace	8.4	7.2
whole, raw	1, size 2 [61g]	90	trace	7.6	6.6
whole, raw	1, size 3 [57g]	84	trace	7.1	6.2
whole, raw	1, size 4 [47g]	69	trace	5.9	5.1
yolk, raw	100g	339	trace	16.1	30.5

159

SPECIFIC	AMOUNT	KCALS	CARB	PROT	FAT
Duck egg					
whole, raw	100g	163	trace	14.3	11.8
whole, raw	1, average [75g]	122	trace	17.2	14.2
Egg-based dessert					
Meringue, with cream	100g	376	40.0	3.3	23.6
Meringue, with cream	1 [28g]	105	11.2	0.9	6.6
Meringue, without cream	100g	379	95.4	5.3	trace
Meringue, without cream	1 [8g]	30	7.6	0.4	trace
Egg-based dish					
Egg fried rice	100g	208	25.7	4.2	10.6
Egg-fried rice	300g portion	624	77.1	12.6	31.8
Omelette, cheese	100g	266	trace	15.9	22.6
Omelette, cheese	2 egg omelette [180g]	479	trace	28.6	40.7
Omelette, plain	100g	191	trace	10.9	16.4
Omelette, plain	2 egg omelette [120g]	229	trace	13.1	19.7
Quiche, cheese and egg	100g	314	17.3	12.5	22.2
Quiche, cheese and egg	70g slice	220	12.1	8.8	15.5
Quiche, cheese and egg	120g slice	377	20.8	15.0	26.6
Quiche, cheese and egg	190g slice	597	32.9	23.8	42.2
Quiche, cheese and egg, wholemeal	100g	308	14.5	13.2	22.4

Specific	Amount	Kcals	Carb	Prot	Fat
Quiche, cheese and egg, wholemeal	70g slice	216	10.2	9.2	15.7
Quiche, cheese and egg, wholemeal	120g slice	370	17.4	15.8	26.9
Quiche, cheese and egg, wholemeal	190g slice	585	27.6	25.1	42.6
Scotch egg	100g	251	13.1	12.0	17.1
Scotch egg	1, average [120g]	301	15.7	14.4	20.5

MILK AND DAIRY PRODUCTS

SPECIFIC	AMOUNT	KCALS	CARB	PROT	FAT
Butter	100g	737	trace	0.5	81.7
	thin spreading for bread [7g]	52	trace	trace	2.9
	thick spreading for bread [12g]	88	trace	0.1	9.8
	restaurant portion [20g]	147	trace	0.1	16.3
Cheese					
Brie	55g portion	98	1.7	5.1	8.0
Brie	100g	319	trace	19.3	26.9
Brie	40g portion	128	trace	7.7	10.8
Camembert	100g	297	trace	20.9	23.7
Camembert	40g portion	119	trace	8.4	9.5
Cheddar, average	100g	412	0.1	25.5	34.4
Cheddar, average	20g portion	82.4	trace	5.1	6.9
Cheddar, average	40g portion	165	trace	10.2	13.8
Cheddar, average	60g portion	247	0.1	15.3	20.6
Cheddar, vegetarian	100g	425	trace	25.8	35.7
Cheddar, vegetarian	40g portion	170	trace	10.3	14.3

Specific	Amount	Kcals	Carb	Prot	Fat
Cheddar-type, reduced fat	100g	261	trace	31.5	15.0
Cheddar-type, reduced fat	40g portion	104	trace	12.6	6.0
Cheese spread	100g	276	4.4	13.5	22.8
Cheese spread	40g portion	110	1.8	5.4	9.1
Cottage cheese, plain	100g	98	2.1	13.8	3.9
Cottage cheese, plain	112g pot	110	2.4	2.0	4.4
Cottage cheese, reduced fat	100g	78	3.3	13.3	1.4
Cottage cheese, reduced fat	112g pot	87	3.7	1.5	1.6
Cottage cheese, with additions	100g	95	2.6	12.8	3.8
Cottage cheese, with additions	112g pot	106	2.9	14.3	4.3
Cream cheese	100g	439	trace	3.1	47.4
Cream cheese	30g portion for bread	132	trace	0.9	14.2
Danish Blue	100g	347	trace	20.1	29.6
Danish Blue	40g portion	139	trace	8.0	11.8
Edam	100g	333	trace	26.0	25.4
Edam	40g portion	133	trace	10.4	10.2
Feta	100g	250	1.5	15.6	20.2
Feta	20g portion	50	0.3	3.1	4.0
Fromage Frais, fruit	100g	131	13.8	6.8	5.8
Fromage Frais, fruit	60g pot	79	8.3	4.1	3.5
Fromage Frais, plain	100g	113	5.7	6.8	7.1
Fromage Frais, plain	60g pot	68	3.4	4.1	4.3
Fromage Frais, very low fat	100g	58	6.8	7.7	0.2

164

Specific	Amount	Kcals	Carb	Prot	Fat
Fromage Frais, very low fat	60g pot	35	4.1	4.6	0.1
Gouda	100g	375	trace	24.0	31.0
Gouda	40g portion	150	trace	9.6	12.4
Hard cheese, average	100g	405	0.1	24.7	34.0
Hard cheese, average	40g portion	162	trace	9.9	13.6
Lymeswold	100g	425	trace	15.6	40.3
Lymeswold	40g portion	170	trace	6.2	16.1
Parmesan	100g	452	trace	39.4	32.7
Parmesan	10g portion	45	trace	3.9	3.3
Processed, plain	100g	330	0.9	20.8	27.0
Processed, plain	20g slice	66	0.2	4.2	5.4
Soft cheese, full fat	100g	313	trace	8.6	31.0
Soft cheese, full fat	55g portion	172	trace	4.7	17.1
Soft cheese, medium fat	100g	179	3.1	9.2	14.5
Stilton	100g	411	0.1	22.7	35.5
Stilton	40g portion	164	trace	9.1	14.2
White, average	100g	376	0.1	23.4	31.3
White, average	40g portion	150	trace	9.4	12.5
Cream, fresh					
clotted	100g	586	2.3	1.6	63.5
clotted	small carton [150g]	879	3.5	2.4	95.3
double	100g	449	2.7	1.7	48.0

SPECIFIC	AMOUNT	KCALS	CARB	PROT	FAT
double	small carton [150g]	674	4.1	2.6	72.0
half	100g	148	4.3	3.0	13.3
half	small carton [150g]	222	6.5	4.5	20.0
single	100g	198	4.1	2.6	19.1
single	small carton [150g]	297	6.2	3.9	28.7
soured	100g	205	3.8	2.9	19.9
soured	small carton [150g]	308	5.7	4.4	30.0
whipping	100g	373	3.1	2.0	39.3
whipping	small carton [150g]	560	4.7	3.0	59.0
Cream, imitation					
Dessert Top	100g	291	6.0	2.4	28.8
Dessert Top	15g portion for dessert	43.7	0.9	0.4	4.3
Dream Topping, made with semi-skimmed milk	100g	166	12.2	3.9	11.7
Dream Topping, made with semi-skimmed milk	15g portion for dessert	25	1.8	0.6	1.8
Dream Topping, made with whole milk	100g	182	12.1	3.8	13.5
Dream Topping, made with whole milk	15g portion for dessert	27	1.8	0.6	2.0
Elmlea, double	15g portion for dessert	68	0.5	0.4	7.2
Elmlea, double	100g	454	3.2	2.5	48.0

SPECIFIC	AMOUNT	KCALS	CARB	PROT	FAT
Elmlea, single	100g	190	4.1	3.2	18.0
Elmlea, single	15g portion for dessert	28.5	0.6	0.5	2.7
Elmlea, whipping	100g	319	3.2	2.5	33.0
Elmlea, whipping	15g portion for dessert	48	0.5	0.4	5.0
Tip Top	100g	110	8.5	5.0	6.5
Tip Top	15g portion for dessert	17	1.3	0.8	1.0
Cream, sterilised					
canned	100g	239	3.7	2.5	23.9
canned	15g portion for dessert	36	0.6	0.4	3.6
Cream, Uht					
canned spray	100g	309	3.5	1.9	32.0
canned spray	15g portion for dessert	46.4	0.5	0.3	4.8
Dairy/Fat spread	100g	662	trace	0.4	73.4
	medium spreading for bread [10g]	66	trace	trace	7.3
Dessert					
Cheesecake	100g	242	33.0	5.7	10.6
Cheesecake	110g slice	266	36.3	6.3	11.7

Specific	Amount	Kcals	Carb	Prot	Fat
Custard, made with skimmed milk	100g	79	16.8	3.8	0.1
Custard, made with skimmed milk	150g portion	119	25.2	5.7	0.2
Custard, made with whole milk	100g	117	16.6	3.7	4.5
Custard, made with whole milk	150g portion	176	25	5.6	6.8
Instant dessert, made with skimmed milk	100g	97	14.9	3.1	3.2
Instant dessert, made with skimmed milk	120g portion	116	17.9	3.7	3.8
Instant dessert, made with whole milk	100g	125	14.8	3.1	6.3
Instant dessert, made with whole milk	120g portion	150	22.2	4.7	9.5
Milk pudding, made with skimmed milk	100g	93	20.1	4.0	0.2
Milk pudding, made with skimmed milk	200g portion	186	40.2	8.0	0.4
Milk pudding, made with whole milk	100g	129	19.9	3.9	4.3

Specific	Amount	Kcals	Carb	Prot	Fat
Milk pudding, made with whole milk	200g portion	258	39.8	7.8	8.6
Mousse, chocolate	100g	139	19.9	4.0	5.4
Mousse, chocolate	60g pot	83	11.9	2.4	3.2
Mousse, fruit	100g	137	18.0	4.5	5.7
Mousse, fruit	60g pot	82.2	10.8	2.7	3.4
Rice pudding, canned	100g	89	14.0	3.4	2.5
Rice pudding, canned	200g portion	178	28.0	6.8	5.0
Trifle, home-made	100g	160	22.3	3.6	6.3
Trifle, home-made	170g portion	272	37.9	6.1	10.7
Trifle, home-made, with fresh cream	100g	166	19.5	2.4	9.2
Trifle, home-made, with fresh cream	170g portion	282	33.2	4.1	15.6
Ice cream					
Choc ice	100g	277	28.1	3.5	17.5
Choc ice	50g bar	139	14.1	1.8	8.8
Cornetto	100g	260	34.5	3.7	12.9
Cornetto	75g cone	195	25.9	2.8	9.6
Dairy, flavoured	100g	179	24.7	3.5	8.0
Dairy, flavoured	60g portion	107	14.8	2.1	4.8
Dairy, vanilla	100g	194	24.4	3.6	9.8

Specific	Amount	Kcals	Carb	Prot	Fat
Dairy, vanilla	60g portion	116	14.6	2.2	5.9
Lemon sorbet	100g	131	34.2	0.9	trace
Lemon sorbet	60g portion	6.6	20.5	0.5	trace
Non-dairy, flavoured	100g	166	23.2	3.1	7.4
Non-dairy, flavoured	60g portion	10	13.9	1.9	4.4
Non-dairy, vanilla	100g	178	23.1	3.2	8.7
Non-dairy, vanilla	60g portion	107	13.9	1.9	5.1
Ice cream dessert					
Arctic roll	100g	200	33.3	4.1	6.6
Arctic roll	70g slice	140	23.3	2.9	4.6
assorted, average	100g	227	22.8	3.3	14.2
assorted, average	45g portion	102	10.3	1.5	6.4
Chocolate nut sundae	100g	278	34.2	3.0	15.3
Chocolate nut sundae	70g portion	195	23.9	2.1	10.7
Ice cream mix					
prepared	100g	182	25.1	4.1	7.9
Milk, condensed					
skimmed, sweetened	100g	267	60.0	10.0	0.2
whole, sweetened	100g	333	55.5	8.5	10.1

SPECIFIC	AMOUNT	KCALS	CARB	PROT	FAT
Milk, dried					
skimmed	100g	348	52.9	36.1	0.6
skimmed, with vegetable fat	100g	487	42.6	23.3	25.9
Milk, evaporated					
whole	100g	151	8.5	8.4	9.4
whole	170g can	257	14.5	14.3	16.0
Milk, flavoured					
mixed flavours, skimmed	100g	68	10.6	3.6	1.5
mixed flavours, skimmed	1/2 pint [293g]	199	31.1	10.6	4.4
Milk, goat's					
pasteurised	100g	60	4.4	3.1	3.5
pasteurised	1 pint [585g]	351	25.7	18.1	20.5
Milk, semi-skimmed					
pasteurised	100g	46	5.0	3.3	1.6
pasteurised	1 pint [585g]	269	29.3	19.3	9.4
pasteurised	30g portion for tea/coffee	14	1.5	1.0	0.5
fortified plus smp	100g	51	5.8	3.7	1.6
fortified plus smp	1 pint [585g]	2988	33.9	21.6	9.4

171

SPECIFIC	AMOUNT	KCALS	CARB	PROT	FAT
Uht	100g	46	4.8	3.3	1.7
Uht	1 pint [585g]	269	28.1	19.3	9.9
Milk, sheep's					
raw	100g	95	5.1	5.4	6.0
raw	1 pint [585g]	556	29.8	31.6	35.1
pasteurised	100g	33	5.0	3.3	0.1
pasteurised	1 pint [585g]	193	29.3	19.3	0.
Milk, skimmed					
pasteurised	30g portion for tea or coffee	10	1.5	1.0	trace
fortified plus smp	100g	39	6.0	3.8	0.1
fortified plus smp	1 pint [585g]	228	35.1	22.2	0.6
Uht, fortified	100g	35	5.0	3.5	0.2
Milk, soya					
plain	100g	32	0.8	2.9	1.9
plain	1 pint [585g]	187	4.7	17.0	11.1
flavoured	100g	40	3.6	2.8	1.7
flavoured	1 pint [585g]	23	21.1	16.4	9.

SPECIFIC	AMOUNT	KCALS	CARB	PROT	FAT
Milk, whole					
pasteurised	100g	66	4.8	3.2	3.9
pasteurised	1 pint [585g]	386	28.1	18.7	22.8
pasteurised	30g portion for tea or coffee	20	1.4	1.0	1.2
sterilised	100g	66	4.5	3.5	3.9
sterilised	1 pint [585g]	386	26.3	20.5	22.8
Uht, fortified	1 pint [585g]	205	29.3	20.5	1.2
Yoghurt					
drinking	100g	62	13.1	3.1	trace
drinking	210g [200ml] carton	130	27.5	6.5	trace
Greek, cows	100g	115	2.0	6.4	9.1
Greek, cow's	150g carton	173	3.0	9.6	13.7
Greek, sheep's	100g	106	5.6	4.4	7.5
Greek, sheep's	150g carton	159	8.4	6.6	11.3
Low calorie	100g	41	6.0	4.3	0.2
Low calorie	150g carton	61.5	9.0	6.5	0.3
Low fat, flavoured	100g	90	17.9	3.8	0.9
Low fat, flavoured	150g carton	135	26.9	5.7	1.4
Low fat, fruit	100g	90	17.9	4.1	0.7
Low fat, fruit	150g carton	135	26.9	6.2	1.1
Low fat, plain	100g	56	7.5	5.1	0.8

173

Specific	Amount	Kcals	Carb	Prot	Fat
Low fat, plain	150g carton	84	11.3	7.7	1.2
Soya	100g	72	3.9	5.0	4.2
Soya	150g carton	108	5.9	7.5	6.3
Whole milk, fruit	150g carton	158	23.6	7.7	4.2
Whole milk, fruit	100g	105	15.7	5.1	2.8
Whole milk, plain	100g	79	7.8	5.7	3.0
Whole milk, plain	150g carton	119	11.7	8.6	4.5
Yoghurt-based dish					
Tzatziki	100g	66	2.0	3.7	4.9

MEAT AND MEAT PRODUCTS

SPECIFIC	AMOUNT	KCALS	CARB	PROT	FAT
Bacon					
Collar joint, boiled	100g	325	0	20.4	27.0
Collar joint, boiled	55g portion	179	0	11.2	14.9
Collar joint, raw	100g	319	0	14.6	28.9
Gammon joint, boiled	100g	269	0	24.7	18.9
Gammon joint, boiled	55g portion	148	0	13.6	10.4
Gammon joint, raw	100g	236	0	17.6	18.3
Gammon rasher, grilled	100g	228	0	29.5	12.2
Gammon rasher, grilled	55g portion	125	0	16.2	6.7
Rasher [back], grilled	100g	405	0	25.3	33.8
Rasher [back], grilled	1 rasher [25g]	101	0	6.3	8.5
Rasher [back], raw	100g	428	0	14.2	41.2
Rasher [middle], grilled	100g	416	0	24.9	35.1
Rasher [middle], grilled	1 rasher [40g]	166	0	10.0	14.0
Rasher [middle], raw	100g	425	0	14.3	40.9
Rasher [streaky], grilled	100g	422	0	24.5	36.0
Rasher [streaky], grilled	1 rasher [20g]	84	0	4.9	7.2
Rasher [streaky], raw	100g	414	0	14.6	39.5

175

SPECIFIC	AMOUNT	KCALS	CARB	PROT	FAT
Beef					
Brisket, boiled	100g	326	0	27.6	23.9
Brisket, boiled	200g portion	652	0	55.2	47.8
Brisket, raw	100g	252	0	16.8	20.5
Forerib, raw	100g	290	0	16.0	25.1
Forerib, roast	100g	349	0	22.4	28.8
Forerib, roast	120g portion	419	0	26.9	34.6
Mince, raw	100g	221	0	18.8	16.2
Mince, stewed	100g	229	0	23.1	15.2
Mince, stewed	200g portion	458	0	46.2	30.4
Rump steak, fried	100g	246	0	28.6	14.6
Rump steak, fried	115g steak	283	0	32.9	16.8
Rump steak, fried	180g steak	443	0	51.5	26.3
Rump steak, grilled	100g	218	0	27.3	12.1
Rump steak, grilled	115g steak	251	0	31.4	13.9
Rump steak, grilled	180g steak	392	0	49.1	21.8
Rump steak, raw	100g	197	0	18.9	13.5
Salted	100g	119	0	27.1	0.4
Silverside, salted, boiled	100g	242	0	28.6	14.2
Silverside, salted, boiled	125g portion	303	0	35.8	17.8
Sirloin, raw	100g	272	0	16.6	22.8
Sirloin, roast	100g	284	0	23.6	21.1
Sirloin, roast	120g portion	341	0	28.3	25.3

176

SPECIFIC	AMOUNT	KCALS	CARB	PROT	FAT
Stewing steak, raw	100g	176	0	20.2	10.6
Stewing steak, stewed	100g	223	0	30.9	11.0
Stewing steak, stewed	200g portion	446	0	15.5	5.6
Topside, raw	100g	179	0	19.6	11.2
Topside, roast	100g	214	0	26.6	12.0
Topside, roast	120g portion	792	0	31.9	14.4
Beef-based dish					
Beef kheema	100g	413	0.3	18.2	37.7
Beef kheema	250g portion	1032	0.8	45.5	94.3
Beef steak pudding	100g	224	18.8	10.8	12.3
Beef steak pudding	230g portion	515	43.2	24.8	28.3
Beef steak pudding	450g portion	1008	84.6	48.6	55.4
Beef stew, home made	100g	120	4.6	9.7	7.2
Beef stew, home-made	330g portion	396	15.2	32.0	23.8
Bolognese sauce	100g	145	3.7	8.0	11.1
Bolognese sauce	220g portion	319	8.1	17.6	24.4
Chilli con carne	100g	151	8.3	11.0	8.5
Chilli con carne	220g portion	332	18.3	24.2	18.7
Chow mein	100g	136	14.7	6.7	6.0
Chow mein	330g portion	449	48.5	22.1	19.8
Curry	100g	137	6.3	13.5	6.6
Curry	330g portion	452	20.8	44.6	21.8

Specific	Amount	Kcals	Carb	Prot	Fat
Curry with rice	100g	137	16.9	8.8	4.3
Curry with rice	400g portion	548	67.6	35.2	17.2
Stewed steak, canned, with gravy	100g	176	1.0	14.8	12.5
Stewed steak, canned, with gravy	½ can [210g]	370	2.1	31.1	26.3
Beefburgers, frozen, raw	100g	265	5.3	15.2	20.5
Beefburgers, frozen, fried	100g	264	7.0	20.4	17.3
Beefburgers, frozen, fried	1 burger [50g]	132	3.5	10.2	8.7
Corned beef, canned	100g	217	0	26.9	12.1
Chicken					
Breaded, fried in oil	100g	242	14.8	18.0	12.7
Breaded, fried in oil	140g portion	339	20.7	25.2	15.2
Dark meat, boiled	100g	204	0	28.6	9.9
Dark meat, boiled	120g portion	245	0	34.3	11.9
Dark meat, raw	100g	126	0	19.1	5.5
Dark meat, roast	100g	155	0	23.1	6.9
Dark meat, roast	120g portion	186	0	27.7	8.3
Leg quarter, roast	100g	92	0	15.4	3.4
Leg quarter, roast	1 quarter [190g]	175	0	29.3	6.5
Light and dark meat, boiled	100g	183	0	29.2	7.3
Light and dark meat, boiled	120g portion	220	0	35.0	8.8

SPECIFIC	AMOUNT	KCALS	CARB	PROT	FAT
Light and dark meat, raw	100g	121	0	20.5	4.3
Light and dark meat, roast	100g	148	0	24.8	5.4
Light and dark meat, roast	120g portion	178	0	29.8	6.5
Light meat, boiled	100g	163	0	29.7	4.9
Light meat, boiled	120g portion	196	0	35.6	5.9
Light meat, raw	100g	116	0	21.8	3.2
Light meat, roast	100g	142	0	26.5	4.0
Light meat, roast	120g portion	170	0	31.8	4.8
Wing quarter, roast	100g	74	0	12.4	2.7
Wing quarter, roast	1 quarter [190g]	141	0	23.6	5.1
Chicken-based dish					
Chicken in white sauce, canned	100g	176	3.5	9.5	15.0
Chicken in white sauce, canned	420g can	780	15.0	40.0	63.0
Curry	100g	205	3.1	10.2	17.0
Curry	330g portion	677	68.3	83.2	56.1
Curry with rice	100g	144	16.9	7.8	5.5
Curry with rice	330g portion	475	55.8	25.7	18.2
Duck					
raw	100g	122	0	19.7	4.8

179

Specific	Amount	Kcals	Carb	Prot	Fat
roast	100g	189	0	25.3	9.7
roast	120g portion	227	0	30.4	11.6
Goose					
roast	100g	319	0	29.3	22.4
roast	120g portion	383	0	35.2	26.9
Grouse					
roast	100g	173	0	31.3	5.3
roast	1 grouse [160g]	277	0	50.1	8.5
Ham					
canned	100g	120	0	18.4	5.1
canned	120g portion	144	0	22.1	6.1
Honey roast	100g	108	2.4	18.2	2.9
Honey roast	30g slice	32	0.7	5.4	0.9
Smoked	100g	94	0.8	17.6	2.3
Smoked	30g slice	28	0.2	5.9	0.7
Hare					
Stewed	100g	192	0	29.9	8.0
Stewed	150g portion	288	0	44.9	12.0

SPECIFIC	AMOUNT	KCALS	CARB	PROT	FAT
Lamb					
Breast, raw	100g	378	0	16.7	34.6
Breast, roast	100g	410	0	19.1	37.1
breast, roast	120g portion	492	0	22.9	44.5
Chops, Loin, grilled	100g	355	0	23.5	29.0
Chops, Loin, grilled	1 chop [90g]	320	0	21.2	26.1
Chops, Loin, raw	100g	377	0	14.6	35.4
Cutlets, grilled	100g	370	0	23.0	30.9
Cutlets, grilled	1 cutlet [50g]	185	0	11.5	15.5
Cutlets, raw	100g	386	0	14.7	36.3
Leg, raw	100g	240	0	17.9	18.7
Leg, roast	100g	266	0	26.1	17.9
Leg, roast	120g portion	319	0	31.2	21.5
Scrag and neck, raw	100g	316	0	15.6	28.2
Scrag and neck, stewed	100g	292	0	25.6	21.1
Scrag and neck, stewed	200g portion	598	0	51.2	42.2
Shoulder, raw	100g	314	0	15.6	28.0
Shoulder, roast	100g	316	0	19.9	26.3
Shoulder, roast	120g portion	379	0	23.9	50.0
Irish stew	100g	123	9.1	5.3	7.6
Irish stew	330g portion	406	30.0	17.5	25.1
Lamb kheema	100g	328	2.3	14.6	29.1
Lamb kheema	250g portion	820	5.8	36.5	72.8

SPECIFIC	AMOUNT	KCALS	CARB	PROT	FAT
Moussaka	100g	184	7.0	9.1	13.6
Moussaka	330g portion	607	23.1	30.0	44.9
Lamb hot pot, frozen	100g	92	7.9	7.9	3.4
Lamb hot pot, frozen	340g portion	320	28.0	28.0	12.0
Moussaka, frozen	100g	105	9.9	7.0	4.4
Moussaka, frozen	340g portion	355	34.0	24.0	5.4
Meat-based dish					
Cottage pie, frozen	100g	110	11.4	5.1	4.7
Cottage pie, frozen	450g portion	495	51.3	23.0	21.2
Hot pot, home made	100g	114	10.1	9.4	4.5
Hot pot, home, made	330g portion	376	33.3	31.0	14.9
Lasagne	100g	102	12.8	5.0	3.8
Lasagne	450g portion	459	57.6	22.5	17.1
Meat curry	100g	162	9.1	8.5	10.5
Meat curry	330g portion	535	30.0	28.1	34.7
Shepherd's pie	100g	118	8.2	8.0	6.2
Shepherd's pie	300g portion	354	24.6	24.0	18.6
Meat-based products					
Black pudding, fried	100g	305	15.0	12.9	21.9
Black pudding, fried	120g portion [3 slices]	366	18.0	15.5	26.3

Specific	Amount	Kcals	Carb	Prot	Fat
Brawn	100g	153	0	12.4	11.5
Chopped ham and pork, canned	100g	275	1.4	14.4	23.6
Cornish pasty	100g	332	31.1	8.0	20.4
Cornish pasty	1 medium pasty [155g]	515	48.2	12.4	31.6
Faggots	100g	268	15.3	11.1	18.5
Faggots	2 faggots [150g]	402	23.0	16.7	27.8
Frankfurters	100g	274	3.0	9.5	25.0
Frankfurters	1 large [47g]	129	1.4	4.5	11.8
Grillsteaks, grilled	100g	305	0.5	22.1	23.9
Grillsteaks, grilled	1 steak [80g]	244	0.4	17.7	19.1
Haggis, boiled	100g	310	19.2	10.7	21.7
Haggis, boiled	220g portion	682	42.2	23.5	47.7
Liver pate	100g	316	1.0	13.1	28.9
Liver pate	40g portion for bread	126	0.4	5.2	11.6
Liver pate, low fat	100g	191	2.8	18.0	12.0
Liver pate, low fat	40g portion for bread	76	1.1	7.2	4.8
Liver sausage	100g	310	4.3	12.9	26.9
Liver sausage	40g portion for bread	124	1.7	5.2	10.8
Luncheon meat, canned	100g	313	5.5	12.6	26.9
Luncheon meat, canned	20g slice	63	3.3	7.6	16.1
Meat paste	100g	173	3.0	15.2	11.2
Meat paste	40g portion for bread	69	1.2	6.1	4.5

183

Specific	Amount	Kcals	Carb	Prot	Fat
Pepperami	100g	560	1.0	20	52
Pepperami	25g stick	140	0.3	5.0	13
Polony	100g	281	14.2	9.4	21.1
Polony	20g slice	56	2.8	1.9	4.2
Pork pie, individual	100g	376	24.9	9.8	27.0
Pork pie, individual	1 pie [140g]	526	34.9	13.7	37.8
Salami	100g	491	1.9	19.3	45.2
Salami	1 slice [17g]	83	0.3	3.3	7.7
Sausage roll, flaky pastry	100g	477	32.3	7.1	36.4
Sausage roll, flaky pastry	1, medium [60g]	286	19.4	46.3	21.8
Sausage roll, short pastry	100g	459	37.5	8.0	31.9
Sausage roll, short pastry	1, medium [60g]	275	22.5	4.8	19.1
Saveloy	100g	262	10.1	9.9	20.5
Saveloy	1 saveloy [65g]	170	6.6	6.4	1.6
Steak and kidney pie,individual, pastry top and bottom	1 pie [200g]	646	51.2	18.2	42.4
Steak and kidney pie, individual, pastry top and bottom	100g	323	25.6	9.1	21.2
Steak and kidney pie, pastry top only	100g	286	15.9	15.2	18.4
Steak and kidney pie, pastry top only	120g portion	343	19.1	18.2	22.1
White pudding	100g	450	36.3	7.0	31.8
White pudding	120g portion	540	43.6	8.4	38.2
Sausages, beef, fried	100g	269	14.9	12.9	18.0

Specific	Amount	Kcals	Carb	Prot	Fat
Sausages, beef, fried	1 thin sausage [35g]	94	5.2	4.5	6.3
Sausages, beef, fried	1 large [60g]	161	8.9	1.1	10.8
Sausages, beef, grilled	100g	265	15.2	13.0	17.3
Sausages, beef, grilled	1 large sausage [60g]	159	9.1	7.8	10.4
Sausages, beef, grilled	1 thin sausage [35g]	93	5.3	4.6	6.1
Sausages, beef, raw	100g	299	11.7	9.6	24.1
Sausages, pork, fried	100g	317	11.0	13.8	24.5
Sausages, pork, fried	1 thin sausage [35g]	111	3.9	4.8	8.6
Sausages, pork, fried	1 large sausage [60g]	190	6.6	8.3	14.7
Sausages, pork, grilled	100g	318	11.5	13.3	24.6
Sausages, pork, grilled	1 thin sausage [35g]	111	4.0	4.7	8.6
Sausages, pork, grilled	1 large sausage [60g]	191	6.9	8.0	14.8
Sausages, pork, low fat, fried	100g	211	9.1	14.9	13.0
Sausages, pork, low fat, fried	1 thin sausage [35g]	73.9	3.2	5.2	4.6
Sausages, pork, low fat, fried	1 large sausage [60g]	127	5.5	8.9	7.8
Sausages, pork, low fat, grilled	100g	229	10.8	16.2	13.8
Sausages, pork, low fat, grilled	1 thin sausage [35g]	80	3.8	5.7	4.8
Sausages, pork, low fat, grilled	1 large sausage [60g]	137	6.5	9.7	8.3
Sausages, pork, low fat, raw	100g	166	8.1	12.5	9.5
Sausages, pork, raw	100g	367	9.5	10.6	32.1
Mutton-based dish					
Mutton biriani	100g	276	25.1	7.5	16.9

Specific	Amount	Kcals	Carb	Prot	Fat
Mutton biriani	330g portion	911	82.8	24.8	55.8
Mutton curry	100g	374	3.9	14.9	33.4
Mutton curry	330g portion	1234	12.9	49.2	110.2
Offal					
Heart, lamb, raw	100g	119	0	17.1	5.6
Heart, ox, raw	100g	108	0	18.9	3.6
Heart, ox, stewed	100g	179	0	31.4	5.9
Heart, sheep, roast	100g	237	0	26.1	14.7
Kidney, lamb, fried	100g	155	0	24.6	6.3
Kidney, lamb, fried	1 whole kidney [90g]	140	0	22.1	5.7
Kidney, lamb,raw	100g	90	0	16.5	2.7
Kidney, ox, raw	100g	86	0	15.7	2.6
Kidney, ox, stewed	100g	172	0	25.6	7.7
Kidney, ox, stewed	112g portion	193	0	28.7	8.6
Kidney, pig, raw	100g	90	0	16.3	2.7
Kidney, pig, stewed	100g	153	0	24.4	6.1
Kidney, pig, stewed	112g portion	171	0	27.3	6.8
Liver, calf, coated in flour and fried	100g	254	7.3	26.9	13.2
Liver, calf, coated in oil and fried	40g slice	102	2.9	10.8	5.3
Liver, calf, raw	100g	153	1.9	20.1	7.3
Liver, chicken, coated in flour and fried	100g	194	3.4	20.7	10.9
Liver, chicken, coated in flour and fried	70g portion	136	2.4	14.5	7.6

SPECIFIC	AMOUNT	KCALS	CARB	PROT	FAT
Liver, chicken, raw	100g	135	0.6	19.1	6.3
Liver, lamb, coated in flour and fried	100g	232	3.9	22.9	14.0
Liver, lamb, coated in oil and fried	40g slice	93	1.6	9.2	16.8
Liver, lamb, raw	100g	179	1.6	20.1	10.3
Liver, ox raw	100g	163	2.2	21.1	7.8
Liver, ox, coated in flour and stewed	100g	198	3.6	24.8	9.5
Liver, ox, coated in flour and stewed	70g portion	139	2.5	17.4	6.7
Liver, pig, coated in flour and stewed	100g	189	3.6	25.6	8.1
Liver, pig, coated in flour and stewed	70g portion	132	2.5	17.9	5.7
Liver, pig, raw	100g	154	2.1	21.3	6.8
Oxtail, stewed	100g	243	0	30.5	13.4
Oxtail, stewed	330g portion	8126	0	100.7	44.2
Sweetbread, lamb, coated in egg and breadcrumbs and fried	100g	230	5.6	19.4	14.6
Sweetbread, lamb, coated in egg and breadcrumbs and fried	70g portion	161	3.9	13.6	10.2
Sweetbread, lamb, raw	100g	131	0	15.3	7.8
Tongue, lamb, raw	100g	193	0	15.3	14.6
Tongue, ox, boiled	100g	293	0	19.5	23.9
Tongue, ox, pickled, raw	100g	220	0	15.7	17.5
Tongue, sheep, stewed	100g	289	0	18.2	24.0
Tripe, dressed	100g	60	0	9.4	2.5
Tripe, dressed, stewed in milk	100g	100	0	14.8	4.5

187

Specific	Amount	Carb	Kcals	Prot	Fat
Tripe, dressed, stewed in milk	70g portion	0	70	10.4	3.2
Partridge					
roast	100g	0	212	36.7	7.2
roast	1 partridge [260g]	0	551	95.4	18.7
Pheasant					
roast	100g	0	213	32.2	9.3
roast	1 pheasant [430g]	0	916	138.5	40.0
Pigeon					
roast	100g	0	230	27.8	13.2
roast	1 pigeon [115g]	0	265	32.0	15.2
Pork					
Belly rashers, grilled	100g	0	398	21.1	34.8
Belly rashers, grilled	110g portion	0	438	23.2	38.3
Belly rashers, raw	100g	0	381	15.3	35.5
Chops, Loin, grilled	100g	0	332	28.5	24.2
Chops, Loin, grilled	120g portion	0	398	34.2	29.0
Chops, Loin, raw	100g	0	329	15.9	29.5
Leg, raw	100g	0	269	16.6	22.5
Leg, roast	100g	0	286	26.9	19.8

Specific	Amount	Kcals	Carb	Prot	Fat
Leg, roast	120g portion	343	0	32.3	23.8
Trotters and tails, boiled	100g	280	0	19.8	22.3
Rabbit					
raw	100g	124	0	21.9	4.0
stewed	100g	179	0	27.3	7.7
stewed	200g portion	358	0	54.6	15.4
Tongue					
canned	100g	213	0	16.0	16.5
Turkey					
Dark meat, raw	100g	114	0	20.3	3.6
Dark meat, roast	100g	148	0	27.8	4.1
Dark meat, roast	120g portion	178	0	33.4	4.9
Light and dark meat, raw	100g	107	0	21.9	2.2
Light and dark meat, roast	100g	140	0	28.8	2.7
Light and dark meat, roast	120g portion	168	0	34.6	3.2
Light meat, raw	100g	103	0	23.2	1.1
Light meat, roast	100g	132	0	29.8	1.4
Light meat, roast	120g portion	158	0	35.8	1.7

SPECIFIC	AMOUNT	KCALS	CARB	PROT	FAT
Turkey-based product					
Turkey with ham	100g	123	2.2	19.2	4.1
Turkey with ham	30g slice	37	0.7	5.8	1.2
Veal					
Cutlet, coated in egg and breadcrumbs and fried	100g	215	4.4	31.4	8.1
Cutlet, coated in egg and breadcrumbs and fried	1 cutlet [150g]	323	6.6	47.1	12.2
Fillet, raw	100g	109	0	21.1	2.7
Fillet, roast	100g	230	0	31.6	11.5
Fillet, roast	120g portion	276	0	37.9	13.8
Venison					
Haunch, roast	100g	198	0	35.0	6.4
Haunch, roast	120g portion	238	0	42.0	7.7

FISH, SEAFOOD AND FISH PRODUCTS

SPECIFIC	AMOUNT	KCALS	CARB	PROT	FAT
Anchovies					
canned in oil, drained	100g	280	0	25.2	19.9
canned in oil, drained	1 anchovy [3g]	8.4	0	0.8	0.6
canned in oil, drained	50g tin	140	0	12.6	10.0
canned in oil, drained	average on pizza [10g]	28	0	2.5	2.0
Cockles					
boiled	100g	48	trace	11.3	0.3
boiled	1 cockle [4g]	2	0	0.5	trace
boiled	142g jar	68	0	16.0	0.4
boiled	25g portion	12	0	2.8	0.1
Cod					
dried, salted, boiled	100g	138	0	32.5	0.9
Fillets, baked, with butter added	100g	96	0	21.4	1.2
Fillets, baked, with butter added	50g portion	48	0	10.7	0.6
Fillets, baked, with butter added	120g portion	115	0	25.7	1.4
Fillets, baked, with butter added	175g portion	168	0	37.5	2.1

191

SPECIFIC	AMOUNT	KCALS	CARB	PROT	FAT
Fillets, poached in milk with butter added	100g	94	0	20.9	1.1
Fillets, poached in milk with butter added	50g portion	47	0	10.5	106
Fillets, poached in milk with butter added	120g portion	113	0	25.1	1.3
Fillets, poached in milk with butter added	175g portion	165	0	36.6	1.9
Fillets, raw	100g	76	0	17.4	0.7
in batter, fried in blended oil	100g	199	7.5	19.6	10.3
in batter, fried in dripping	100g	199	7.5	19.6	10.3
in batter, fried in oil or dripping	120g portion	239	9.0	23.5	12.4
in batter, fried in oil or dripping	180g portion	358	13.5	35.3	18.5
in batter, fried in oil or dripping	225g portion	448	16.9	44.1	23.2
Steaks, frozen, raw,	100g	68	0	15.6	0.6
Crab					
boiled	100g	127	0	20.1	5.2
boiled	1 tbsp crabmeat [40g]	51	0	8.0	2.1
canned	100g	81	0	18.1	0.9

SPECIFIC	AMOUNT	KCALS	CARB	PROT	FAT
canned	1 small can [85g]	69	0	15.4	0.8
canned	1 large can [170g]	138	0	30.8	1.5
Dogfish					
in batter, fried	large portion [250g]	663	19.3	41.8	47.0
in batter, fried in blended oil	100g	265	7.7	16.7	18.8
in batter, fried in dripping	100g	265	7.7	16.7	18.8
in batter, fried in oil or dripping	small portion [150g]	400	11.6	25.1	28.2
in batter, fried in oil or dripping	medium portion [200g]	530	15.4	33.4	37.6
Fish fingers					
fried in blended oil	100g	233	17.2	13.5	12.7
fried in lard	100g	233	17.2	13.5	12.7
fried in oil or lard	1 fish finger [28g]	65	4.8	3.8	3.6
fried in oil or lard	1 jumbo size fish finger [60g]	140	10.3	8.1	7.6
grilled	100g	214	19.3	15.1	9.0
grilled	1 fish finger [28g]	60	5.4	4.3	2.5
grilled	1 jumbo size fish finger [60g]	128	11.6	9.1	5.4
Fish-based dish					
Fish pie, home-made	100g	105	12.3	8.0	3.0

Specific	Amount	Kcals	Carb	Prot	Fat
Fish pie, home-made	250g portion	263	30.8	20	7.5
Kedgeree, home-made	100g	166	10.5	14.2	7.9
Kedgeree, home-made	300g portion	498	31.5	42.6	23.7
Fish-based product					
Fish cakes, fried	100g	188	15.1	9.1	10.5
Fish cakes, fried	1 fish cake [50g]	94	7.6	4.6	5.3
Fish paste	100g	169	3.7	15.3	10.4
Fish paste	medium jar [53g]	90	2.0	8.1	0.7
Fish paste	10g portion for bread	17	0.4	1.5	1.0
Taramasalata	100g	446	4.1	3.2	46.4
Taramasalata	1 tbsp [45g]	201	1.8	1.4	20.9
Haddock					
fillet, raw	100g	73	0	16.8	0.6
in breadcrumbs, fried in blended oil	100g	174	3.6	21.4	8.3
in breadcrumbs, fried in dripping	100g	174	3.6	21.4	8.3
in breadcrumbs, fried in oil or dripping	small portion [85g]	148	3.1	18.2	7.1
in breadcrumbs, fried in oil or dripping	medium portion [120g]	209	4.3	25.7	10.0
in breadcrumbs, fried in oil or dripping	large portion [170g]	296	6.1	36.4	12.1
middle cut, steamed	100g	98	0	22.8	0.8
middle cut, steamed	85g portion	83	0	19.4	0.7
smoked, steamed	100g	101	0	23.3	0.9

Specific	Amount	Kcals	Carb	Prot	Fat
smoked, steamed	85g portion	86	5.2	19.8	0.8
middle cut, steamed	100g	98	0	22.8	0.8
Halibut					
middle cut, steamed	85g portion	83	0	19.4	0.7
raw	100g	92	0	17.7	2.4
Herring					
fried in oatmeal	100g	234	1.5	23.1	15.1
fried in oatmeal	85g portion	199	1.3	19.6	12.8
fried in oatmeal	119g portion	278	1.8	27.5	18.0
grilled	100g	135	0	13.9	8.8
grilled	85g portion	115	0	11.8	7.5
grilled	119g portion	161	0	16.5	10.5
raw	100g	234	0	16.8	18.5
Kipper					
baked	100g	205	0	25.5	11.4
baked	125g portion	256	0	31.9	13.7
Lemon sole					
in breadcrumbs, fried	100g	216	9.3	16.1	13.0
in breadcrumbs, fried	small portion [90g]	194	8.4	14.5	11.7

Specific	Amount	Kcals	Carb	Prot	Fat
in breadcrumbs, fried	medium portion [150g]	324	14.0	24.1	19.5
in breadcrumbs, fried	large portion [220g]	475	20.5	35.4	28.6
raw	100g	81	0	17.1	1.4
steamed	100g	91	0	20.6	0.9
steamed	small portion [90g]	81	0	18.5	0.8
steamed	medium portion [150g]	137	0	30.9	1.4
steamed	large portion [220g]	200	0	45.3	2.0
Lobster					
boiled	100g	119	0	22.1	3.4
boiled	2 tbsp lobster meat [85g]	101	0	18.8	2.9
Mackerel					
fried	100g	188	0	21.5	11.3
fried	220g portion	414	0	47.3	28.3
raw	100g	223	0	19.0	16.3
smoked	100g	354	0	18.9	30.9
smoked	150g portion	531	0	28.4	46.4
Mussels					
boiled	100g	87	trace	17.2	2.0

SPECIFIC	AMOUNT	KCALS	CARB	PROT	FAT
boiled	1 mussel, no shell [7g]	6.1	trace	1.2	0.1
boiled	average portion, no shells [40g]	35	trace	6.9	0.8
Pilchards					
in tomato sauce, canned	100g	126	0.7	18.8	5.4
in tomato sauce, canned	1 pilchard [55g]	69.3	0.4	10.3	3.0
in tomato sauce, canned	215g can	271	1.5	40.4	11.6
Plaice					
in batter, fried in blended oil	100g	279	14.4	15.8	18.0
in batter, fried in dripping	100g	279	14.4	15.8	18.0
in batter, fried in oil or dripping	small portion [150g]	419	21.6	23.7	27.0
in batter, fried in oil or dripping	medium portion [200g]	558	28.8	31.6	36
in batter, fried in oil or dripping	large portion [250g]	698	36.0	395.0	45
in bread-crumbs, fried	100g	228	8.6	18.0	13.7
in breadcrumbs, fried	small portion [90g]	205	7.7	16.2	12.3
in breadcrumbs, fried	medium portion [150g]	342	12.9	27.0	20.6
in breadcrumbs, fried	large portion [200g]	456	17.2	36	27.4
raw	100g	91	0	17.9	2.2
steamed	100g	93	0	18.9	1.9
steamed	small portion [75g]	70	0	14.2	1.4
steamed	medium portion [130g]	121	0	24.6	2.5

197

Specific	Amount	Kcals	Carb	Prot	Fat
steamed	large portion [180g]	167	0	34.0	3.4
Prawns					
boiled	100g	107	0	22.6	1.8
boiled	1 prawn, no shell [3g]	3	0	0.7	0.1
boiled	average portion, no shell [60g]	64	0	13.6	1.1
boiled	portion for prawn cocktail [40g]	43	0	9.0	0.8
Roe					
Cod, hard, in breadcrumbs, fried	100g	202	3.0	20.9	11.9
Cod, hard, in breadcrumbs, fried	116g portion	234	3.5	24.2	13.8
Herring, soft, rolled in flour and fried	100g	244	4.7	21.1	15.8
Herring, soft, rolled in flour and fried	85g portion	207	4.0	17.9	13.4
Saithe					
raw	100g	73	0	17.0	0.5
steamed	100g	99	0	23.3	0.6
steamed	130g portion	129	0	30.3	0.8
Salmon					
canned	100g	155	0	20.3	8.2

SPECIFIC	AMOUNT	KCALS	CARB	PROT	FAT
canned	portion for sandwich				
	[40g]	62	0	8.1	3.3
raw	100g	182	0	18.4	12.0
smoked	100g	142	0	25.4	4.5
steamed	100g	197	0	20.1	13.0
Sardines					
in oil, canned, drained	100g	217	0	23.7	13.6
in oil, canned, drained	1 sardine [25g]	54.3	0	5.9	3.4
in oil, canned, drained	portion for sandwich				
	[40g]	109	0	11.9	6.8
in tomato sauce, canned	100g	177	0.5	17.8	11.6
in tomato sauce, canned	portion for sandwich				
	[50g]	89	0.3	8.9	5.8
Scampi					
in breadcrumbs, fried	100g	316	28.9	12.2	17.6
in breadcrumbs, fried	1 piece [15g]	79	7.2	3.1	4.4
in breadcrumbs, fried	150g portion	474	43.4	18.3	26.4
Shrimps					
canned, drained	100g	94	0	20.8	1.2
frozen	100g	73	0	16.5	0.8

Specific	Amount	Kcals	Carb	Prot	Fat
Skate					
in batter, fried	100g	199	4.9	17.9	12.1
in batter, fried	200g portion	398	9.8	35.8	24.2
Squid					
frozen, raw	100g	66	0	13.1	1.5
Trout					
Brown, steamed	100g	135	0	23.5	4.5
Brown, steamed	120g portion	162	0	28.2	5.4
Tuna					
in brine, canned, drained	100g	99	0	23.5	0.6
in brine, canned, drained	portion for sandwich [50g]	45	0	10.6	0.3
	92g portion for salad	91	0	21.6	0.6
in oil, canned, drained	100g	189	0	27.1	9.0
in oil, canned, drained	45g portion for sandwich	85	0	12.2	4.1
in oil, canned, drained	92g portion for salad	174	0	24.9	8.3
Whelks					
boiled, weighed with shell	100g	14	trace	2.8	0.3

Specific	Amount	Kcals	Carb	Prot	Fat
Whitebait					
rolled in flour, fried	100g	525	5.3	19.5	47.5
rolled in flour, fried	1 whitebait [4g]	21	0.2	0.8	1.9
rolled in flour, fried	80g portion	420	4.2	15.6	38
Whiting					
in breadcrumbs, fried	100g	191	7.0	18.1	10.3
in breadcrumbs, fried	180g portion	344	12.6	32.6	18.5
steamed	100g	92	0	20.9	0.9
steamed	85g portion	78	0	17.8	0.8
Winkles					
boiled, weighed with shell	100g	14	trace	2.9	0.3

SWEET AND SAVOURY SNACKS

SPECIFIC	AMOUNT	KCALS	CARB	PROT	FAT
Chocolate Confectionary					
Aero	100g	522	58.3	7.7	28.7
Aero	1 standard bar				
Boost	100g	515	60.1	6.2	27.6
Boost	1 bar [57g]	295	34.3	3.5	15.7
Bounty bar	100g	473	58.3	4.8	26.1
Bounty bar	1 mini bar [30g]	142	17.5	1.44	7.8
Caramac	100g	545	56.3	6.8	32.5
Caramac	1 standard bar	164	16.9	2.1	9.8
Chocolate cream	100g	425	72.6	2.7	13.7
Chocolate cream	1 standard bar [50g]	215	36.3	1.4	6.9
Chocolate, milk	100g	529	59.4	8.4	30.3
Chocolate, milk	50g bar	266	29.7	4.2	15.2
Chocolate, plain	100g	525	64.8	4.7	29.2
Chocolate, plain	50g bar	263	32.4	2.35	14.6
Chocolate, white	100g	529	58.3	8.0	30.9
Chocolate, white	50g bar	265	28.2	4.0	15.5
Chocolates, fancy and filled [assorted]	100g	460	73.3	4.1	18.8
Creme egg	100g	385	58.0	4.1	16.8

SPECIFIC	AMOUNT	KCALS	CARB	PROT	FAT
Creme egg	1 egg [39g]	150	22.6	1.6	6.6
Crunchie	100g	460	72.7	4.6	19.1
Crunchie	1 standard bar	195	30.5	1.9	8.0
Dairy Milk	1 medium bar [54g]	285	30.7	4.3	15.9
Dairy Milk	100g	525	56.8	7.8	29.4
Flake	100g	505	58.4	8.2	28.5
Flake	1 standard bar	170	19.9	2.8	9.7
Fudge	1 standard bar	130	21.6	1.0	5.2
Fudge	100g	420	72.1	3.4	17.2
Kit Kat	100g	499	60.5	8.2	26.6
Kit Kat	2 bars [20g]	100	12.1	1.6	5.3
Mars Bar	100g	441	66.5	5.3	18.9
Mars Bar	1 mini bar [20g]	88	13.3	1.1	3.8
Mars Bar [68g]	300	9.0	0.7	2.6	32.5
Milky Bar	100g	549	55.6	8.4	6.4
Milky Bar	1 medium bar [20g]	110	11.1	1.7	15.8
Milky Way	100g	397	63.4	4.4	8.7
Milky Way	1 standard size [55g]	218	34.8	2.4	17.5
Smarties	100g	456	73.9	5.4	6.3
Smarties	1 tube [36g]	164	26.6	1.9	26.7
Topic	100g	497	56.7	7.4	14.4
Topic	1 bar [54g]	268	30.6	4.0	7.7
Turkish Delight	100g	370	69.0	1.6	

SPECIFIC	AMOUNT	KCALS	CARB	PROT	FAT
Turkish Delight	1 bar [51g]	190	37.8	0.8	3.9
Twirl	100g	525	55.9	8.1	30.1
Twirl	1 finger	115	12.3	1.8	6.6
Twix	100g	480	63.2	5.6	24.5
Twix	50g bar	240	31.6	2.8	12.3
Non-chocolate Confectionary					
Boiled sweets	100g	327	87.3	trace	trace
Fruit Gums	100g	172	44.8	1.0	0
Fruit Gums	1 tube [33g]	57	14.8	0.3	0
Liquorice Allsorts	1 small bag [56g]	175	41.5	2.2	1.2
Liquorice Allsorts	100g	313	74.1	3.9	2.2
Opal Fruits	100g	411	85.3	0.3	7.6
Opal Fruits	1 pack [56g]	230	47.7	0.2	4.3
Pastilles, assorted	100g	253	61.9	5.2	0
Peppermints, assorted	100g	392	102.2	0.5	0.7
Popcorn, candied	100g	480	77.6	2.1	20.0
Popcorn, plain	100g	592	48.6	6.2	42.8
Skittles	100g	383	91.5	0.3	4.3
Skittles	1 pack [60g]	230	54.9	0.2	2.6
Toffees, mixed	100g	430	71.1	2.1	17.2
Toffo	100g	429	69.6	2.3	17.8
Toffo	1 pack [48g]	206	33.4	1.1	8.5

Specific	Amount	Kcals	Carb	Prot	Fat
Turkish Delight	100g	295	77.9	0.6	0
Turkish Delight	50g bar	198	38.9	0.3	0
Savoury Snacks					
Bombay mix	100g	503	35.1	18.8	32.9
Cheddars	100g	534	52.9	11.3	30.2
Corn snacks	100g	519	54.3	7.0	31.9
Peanuts and raisins	100g	435	37.5	15.3	26.0
Potato crisps, assorted	100g	546	49.3	5.6	37.6
Potato crisps, assorted	28g bag	153	13.8	1.6	10.5
Potato crisps, low fat, assorted	100g	456	63.0	6.6	21.5
Potato crisps, low fat, assorted	28g bag	128	17.6	1.8	6.0
Potato Hoops	100g	523	58.5	3.9	32.0
Skips [KP]	100g	512	59.8	4.2	28.4
Skips [KP]	18g bag	92	10.8	0.8	5.1
Tortilla Chips	100g	459	60.1	7.6	22.6
Trail Mix	100g	432	37.2	9.1	28.5
Twiglets	100g	383	62.0	11.3	11.7
Wotsits	100g	545	52.4	9.4	33.1
Wotsits	21g bag	115	11.0	2.0	7.0

SAVOURY DISHES

SPECIFIC	AMOUNT	KCALS	CARB	PROT	FAT
Cereal-based dish					
Pizza, cheese and tomato, home-made	100g	235	24.8	9.0	11.8
Pizza, cheese and tomato, home-made	300g portion	705	74.4	27.0	35.4
Cereal/Vegetable dish					
Pancake roll, with vegetable and beansprout filling	100g	217	20.9	6.6	12.5
Pancake roll, with vegetable and beansprout filling	85g roll	184	17.8	5.6	10.6
Egg-based dish					
Omelette, cheese	100g	266	trace	15.9	22.6
Omelette, cheese	2 eggs [180g]	479	trace	28.6	40.7
Omelette, plain	100g	191	trace	10.9	16.4
Omelette, plain	2 eggs [120g]	229	trace	13.1	19.7
Quiche, cheese and egg	100g	314	17.3	12.5	22.2
Quiche, cheese and egg	70g portion	220	12.1	8.8	15.5
Quiche, cheese and egg	120g portion	377	20.8	15.0	26.6
Quiche, cheese and egg	190g portion	597	32.9	23.8	42.2
Quiche, cheese and egg, wholemeal	100g	308	14.5	13.2	22.4

Specific	Amount	Kcals	Carb	Prot	Fat
Quiche, cheese and egg, wholemeal	70g portion	216	10.2	9.2	15.7
Quiche, cheese and egg, wholemeal	120g portion	370	17.4	15.8	26.9
Quiche, cheese and egg, wholemeal	190g portion	410	27.6	25.1	42.6
Fish-based dish					
Cod fried in batter [chip shop]	100g	199	7.5	19.6	10.3
Cod fried in batter [chip shop]	190g portion	378	14.3	37.2	19.6
Cod fried in batter with chips [chip shop]	190g cod, 200g chips	856	75.3	43.6	44.4
Dogfish in batter	100g	265	7.7	16.7	18.8
Dogfish in batter	190g portion	504	14.6	31.8	35.7
Dogfish in batter	190g dogfish, 200g chips	982	75.6	38.2	60.5
Fish cakes, fried	100g	188	15.1	9.1	10.5
Fish cakes, fried	1 fish cake [50g]	94	7.6	4.6	5.3
Fish fingers, fried	100g	233	17.2	13.5	12.7
Fish fingers, fried	1 fish finger [28g]	65	4.8	3.8	3.6
Fish fingers, fried	1 fish finger, jumbo size [60g]	140	10.3	2.3	1.0
Fish fingers, fried, with home-made chips	3x28g fish fingers, 180g chips	535	68.6	18.4	22.9
Fish fingers, fried, with oven chips	3x28g fish fingers, 180g chips	486	68	17.2	18.4

208

Specific	Amount	Kcals	Carb	Prot	Fat
Fish fingers, grilled	100g	214	19.3	15.1	9.0
Fish fingers, grilled	1 fish finger, [28g]	60	5.4	4.3	2.5
Fish fingers, grilled	! fish finger, jumbo size [60g]	128	11.6	9.1	5.4
Fish fingers, grilled, with oven chips	3x28g fish fingers, 180g chips	471	69.8	18.7	15.1
Fish pie, home-made	100g	105	12.3	8.0	3.0
Fish pie, home-made	250g portion	263	30.8	20.0	7.5
Haddock fried in breadcrumbs	100g	174	3.6	21.4	8.3
Haddock fried in breadcrumbs	120g portion	209	4.3	25.7	10.0
Haddock fried in breadcrumbs with home-made chips	120g haddock, 180g chips	549	58.5	32.7	22.1
Haddock fried in breadcrumbs with oven chips	120g haddock, 180g chips,	500	57.9	31.5	17.6
Plaice fried in batter [chip shop]	100g	279	14.4	15.8	18.0
Plaice fried in batter [chip shop]	190g portion	530	27.4	30.0	34.2
Plaice fried in batter with chips	190g plaice, 200g chips	1008	88.4	36.4	59.0
Scampi, fried in breadcrumbs	100g	316	28.9	12.2	17.6
Scampi, fried in breadcrumbs	150g portion	474	43.4	18.3	26.4
Scampi, fried in breadcrumbs with home-made chips	150g scampi, 180g chips,	814	97.6	25.3	38.5

Specific	Amount	Kcals	Carb	Prot	Fat
Fish/Rice dish					
Kedgeree, home-made	100g	166	10.5	14.2	7.9
Kedgeree, home-made	300g portion	498	31.5	42.6	23.7
Meat-based dish					
Beef chow mein	100g	136	14.7	6.7	6.0
Beef chow mein	330g portion	449	48.5	22.1	19.8
Beef curry	100g	137	6.3	13.5	6.6
Beef curry	330g portion	452	20.8	44.6	21.8
Beef curry with rice	100g	137	16.9	8.8	4.3
Beef curry with rice	400g portion	548	67.6	35.2	17.2
Beef kheema	100g	413	0.3	18.2	37.7
Beef kheema	250g portion	1032	0.8	45.5	94.3
Beef khoftas	100g	353	3.4	23.3	27.6
Beef khoftas	250g portion	883	8.5	58.3	69.0
Beef sausages, fried, with home-made chips	2 x 60g sausages, 180g chips	661	72.1	22.5	33.6
Beef sausages, grilled, with boiled potatoes	2 x 60g sausages, 180g potatoes	448	49.2	18.8	21.0
Beef steak pudding	100g	224	18.8	10.8	12.3
Beef steak pudding	230g portion	515	43.2	24.8	28.3
Beef steak pudding	450g portion	1008	84.6	48.6	5.9

Specific	Amount	Kcals	Carb	Prot	Fat
Beef stew	100g	120	4.6	9.7	7.2
Beef stew	330g portion	396	15.2	32.0	23.8
Beefburger, fried, in burger bun	105g beef-burger, 50g bun	410	31.8	26.0	20.7
Beefburger, fried, in burger bun with french fries	105g beefburger, 50g bun, 93g french fries	670	63.4	29.1	35.1
Bolognese sauce	100g	145	3.7	8.0	11.1
Bolognese sauce	220g portion	319	8.1	17.6	24.4
Chicken curry	100g	205	3.1	10.2	17.0
Chicken curry	330g portion	677	10.2	4.0	56.1
Chicken curry with rice	100g	144	16.9	7.8	5.5
Chicken curry with rice	400g portion	576	67.6	31.2	22.0
Chicken in white sauce	1/2 can [210g]	391	7.4	20.0	31.5
Chicken in white sauce, canned	100g	186	3.5	9.5	15.0
Chilli con carne	100g	151	8.3	11.0	8.5
Chilli con carne	220g portion	332	18.3	24.2	18.7
Cottage pie, frozen	100g	110	11.4	5.1	4.7
Cottage pie, frozen	450g portion	495	51.3	22.9	21.2
Curried meat	100g	162	9.1	8.5	10.5
Curried meat	330g portion	535	30.0	28.1	34.7
Hot pot, home-made	100g	144	10.1	9.4	4.5
Hot pot, home-made	330g portion	475	33.3	31.0	14.9

SPECIFIC	AMOUNT	KCALS	CARB	PROT	FAT
Irish stew	100g	123	9.1	5.3	7.6
Irish stew	330g portion	406	30.0	17.5	25.1
Lamb hot pot, frozen	100g	92	7.9	7.9	3.4
Lamb hot pot, frozen	340g portion	320	28.0	28.0	12.0
Lamb kheema	100g	328	2.3	14.6	29.1
Lamb kheema	250g portion	820	5.8	36.5	72.8
Lasagne	100g	102	12.8	5.0	3.8
Lasagne	450g portion	459	57.6	22.5	17.1
Moussaka, frozen	100g	105	9.9	7.0	4.4
Moussaka, frozen	340g portion	355	34.0	24.0	5.4
Moussaka, home-made	100g	184	7.0	9.1	13.6
Moussaka, home-made	330g portion	607	23.1	30.0	44.9
Mutton biriani	100g	276	25.1	7.5	16.9
Mutton biriani	330g portion	911	82.8	24.8	55.8
Mutton curry	100g	374	3.9	14.9	33.4
Mutton curry	330g portion	1234	12.9	49.2	110.2
Shepherd's pie	100g	118	8.2	8.0	6.2
Shepherd's pie	300g portion	354	24.6	24.0	18.6
Spaghetti bolognese	450g portion [220g sauce, 230g pasta]	558	59.2	25.9	26.0
Steak and kidney pie, individual	100g	323	25.6	9.1	21.2
Steak and kidney pie, individual	1 pie [200g]	646	51.2	18.2	42.4
Steak and kidney pie, pastry top only	100g	286	15.9	15.2	18.4

Specific	Amount	Kcals	Carb	Prot	Fat
Steak and kidney pie, pastry top only	120g portion	343	19.1	18.2	22.1
Pasta dish					
Macaroni cheese with ham, frozen	100g	146	13.3	9.9	5.7
Macaroni cheese with ham, frozen	284g serving	460	42.0	31.0	18.0
Macaroni cheese, home-made	100g	178	13.6	7.3	10.8
Macaroni cheese, home-made	300g portion	534	40.8	21.9	32.4
Rice-based dish					
Egg-fried rice	100g	208	25.7	4.2	10.6
Egg-fried rice	300g portion	624	77.1	12.6	31.8
Risotto, plain	100g	224	34.4	3.0	9.3
Risotto, plain	300g portion	672	103.2	9.0	27.9
Vegetable dish					
Cauliflower cheese	100g	105	5.1	5.9	6.9
Cauliflower cheese	side dish portion [90g]	94.5	4.6	5.3	6.2
Cauliflower cheese	main course portion [200g]	210	10.2	11.8	13.8
Vegetable-based dish					
Ratatouille, canned	100g	38	3.0	1.0	2.5
Ratatouille, canned	1/2 can [200g]	76	6.0	2.0	5.0

Specific	Amount	Kcals	Carb	Prot	Fat
Mixed vegetable chilli, canned	100g	86	9.1	4.3	3.8
Mixed vegetable chilli, canned	$1/_2$ can [200g]	172	18.2	8.6	7.6

DESSERTS

SPECIFIC	AMOUNT	KCALS	CARB	PROT	FAT
Puddings					
Blackcurrant pie					
home-made, pastry top and bottom	100g	262	34.5	3.1	13.3
pastry top and bottom	120g slice	314	41.4	3.7	16.0
Bread pudding					
home-made	100g	297	49.7	5.9	9.6
home-made	190g portion	564	94.4	11.2	18.2
Cheesecake					
frozen, with fruit	100g	242	33.0	5.7	10.6
frozen, with fruit	110g serving	266	36.3	6.3	11.7
individual, fruit puree topping	100g	274	32.4	5.8	13.5
individual, fruit puree topping	90g carton	247	29.2	5.2	12.2
Christmas pudding					
home-made	100g [average portion]	291	49.5	4.6	9.7
retail	100g [average portion]	329	56.3	3.0	11.8

SPECIFIC	AMOUNT	KCALS	CARB	PROT	FAT
Creamed Rice					
canned	100g	91	15.2	3.4	1.8
canned	425g can	387	64.6	14.5	7.7
canned	150g portion	137	22.8	5.1	2.7
Creamed Sago					
canned	100g	82	13.0	2.9	1.8
canned	425g can	349	55.3	12.3	7.7
canned	150g portion	123	19.5	4.4	2.7
Creamed Semolina					
canned	100g	84	13.2	3.6	1.9
canned	425g can	357	56.1	15.3	8.1
canned	150g portion	126	19.8	5.4	2.9
Creme Caramel					
individual	100g	109	20.6	3.0	2.2
individual	128g carton	140	26.4	3.8	2.8
Custard					
Chocolate-flavoured, powdered	100g, powder only	409	82.0	6.0	9.0
Chocolate-flavoured, powdered	1/4 pack serving, made with water	80	16.0	1.2	1.7

Specific	Amount	Kcals	Carb	Prot	Fat
Devon, canned	100g	102	15.8	2.8	3.1
Devon, canned	425g can	434	67.2	11.0	13.2
Devon, canned	150g portion	153	23.7	4.2	4.7
home-made, made with skimmed milk	100g	79	16.8	3.8	0.1
home-made, made with skimmed milk	150g portion	119	25.2	5.7	0.2
home-made, made with whole milk	100g	117	16.6	3.7	4.5
home-made, made with whole milk	150g portion	176	24.9	5.6	6.7
low-fat, canned	100g	75	12.5	3.0	1.4
low-fat, canned	425g can	319	53.1	12.8	6.0
low-fat, canned	150g portion	113	18.8	4.5	2.1
Dessert topping					
Evaporated milk	100g	159	12.0	8.2	9.0
Evaporated milk	1 tbsp [15ml]	24	1.8	1.2	1.4
Tip Top	100g	112	9.0	4.8	6.3
Tip Top	50g serving	56	4.5	2.4	3.7
Frozen dessert					
Arctic roll	100g	200	33.3	4.1	6.6
Arctic roll	70g slice	140	23.3	2.9	4.6
Chocolate nut sundae, individual	100g	278	34.2	3.0	15.3
Chocolate nut sundae, individual	70g sundae	195	23.9	2.1	10.7
Viennetta	100g	272	27.6	3.8	16.4

SPECIFIC	AMOUNT	KCALS	CARB	PROT	FAT
Viennetta	50g slice	136	13.8	1.9	8.2
Frozen ice cream dessert, average	100g	227	22.8	3.3	14.2
Frozen ice cream dessert, average	45g slice	102	10.3	1.5	6.4
Fruit crumble					
Home-made	100g	198	34.0	2.0	6.9
Home-made	170g portion	337	57.8	3.4	11.7
Wholemeal, home-made	100g	193	31.7	2.6	7.1
Wholemeal, home-made	170g portion	328	53.9	4.4	12.1
Fruit pie					
pastry top and bottom	100g	262	34.5	3.1	13.3
pastry top and bottom	120g portion	314	41.4	3.7	16.0
Fruit pie filling					
Apple and blackberry, canned	100g	92	24.1	0.3	trace
Apple and blackberry, canned	385g can	354	92.8	1.2	trace
Black cherry, canned	100g	98	25.8	0.3	trace
Black cherry, canned	400g can	392	103.2	1.2	trace
Ice cream					
Choc ice	100g	277	28.1	3.5	17.5
Cornetto	100g	260	34.5	3.7	12.9

218

Specific	Amount	Kcals	Carb	Prot	Fat
Cornetto	75g cone	195	25.8	2.8	9.7
Dairy, vanilla	100g	194	24.4	3.6	9.8
Dairy, vanilla	60g scoop	116	14.6	2.2	5.9
Flavoured	100g	179	24.7	3.5	8.0
Flavoured	60g scoop	107	14.8	2.1	4.8
Non-dairy, flavoured	100g	166	23.2	3.1	7.4
Non-dairy, flavoured	60g scoop	100	13.9	1.9	4.4
Non-dairy, vanilla	100g	178	23.1	3.2	8.7
Non-dairy, vanilla	60g scoop	107	13.9	1.9	5.2
Ice cream mix	100g	182	25.1	4.1	7.9
Ice cream wafers	100g	342	78.8	10.1	0.7
Instant dessert powder					
Angel delight	100g, powder only	468	73.8	2.3	19.0
Angel delight	1/4 pack serving, made with whole milk	128	13.9	2.9	5.8
Angel delight	1/4 pack serving, made with skimmed milk	104	13.9	2.9	3.2
Average, powder only	100g	391	60.1	2.4	17.3
Average, made with whole milk	100g	125	14.8	3.1	6.3
Average, made with whole milk	120g portion	150	17.8	3.7	7.6
Average, made with skimmed milk	100g	97	14.9	3.1	3.2
Average, made with skimmed milk	120g portion	116	17.9	3.7	3.8

SPECIFIC	AMOUNT	KCALS	CARB	PROT	FAT
Jelly					
Fruit-flavoured, before dilution	100g	280	69.7	4.7	trace
Lemon meringue pie					
Home-made	100g	319	45.9	4.5	14.4
Home-made	120g portion	383	55.1	5.4	17.3
Meringue					
Home-made	100g	379	95.4	5.3	trace
Home-made	1 average [8g]	30	7.6	0.4	trace
Home-made, with cream	100g	376	40.0	3.3	23.6
Home-made, with cream	1 average [28g]	105	11.2	0.9	6.7
Mousse					
Chocolate, individual	100g	139	19.9	4.0	5.4
Chocolate, individual	60g carton	83	11.9	2.4	3.2
Fruit, individual	100g	137	18.0	4.5	5.7
Fruit, individual	60g carton	82.2	10.8	2.7	3.4
Pancakes					
Sweet, made with whole milk	100g	301	35.0	5.9	16.2
Sweet, made with whole milk	110g portion	331	38.5	6.5	17.8

Specific	Amount	Kcals	Carb	Prot	Fat
Pie					
With pie filling	100g	273	34.6	3.2	14.5
With pie filling	120g portion	328	41.5	3.8	17.4
Rice Pudding					
Average, canned	100g	89	14.0	3.4	2.5
Average, canned	200g portion	178	28.0	6.8	5.0
Traditional, with sultanas and nutmeg	100g	101	17.1	3.3	2.6
Traditional, with sultanas and nutmeg	425g can	429	72.7	14.0	11.1
Traditional, with sultanas and nutmeg	150g portion	152	25.7	5.0	3.9
Sorbet					
Lemon, home-made	100g	131	34.2	0.9	trace
Lemon, home-made	60g scoop	79	20.5	0.5	trace
Sponge pudding					
Home-made	100g	340	45.3	5.8	16.3
Home-made	170g portion	578	77.0	9.9	27.7

Specific	Amount	Kcals	Carb	Prot	Fat
Steamed sponge pudding					
Chocolate, with chocolate sauce, canned	100g	299	51.2	2.6	9.3
Chocolate, with chocolate sauce, canned	75g portion	225	38.4	2.0	7.0
Treacle, canned	100g	301	51.4	2.2	9.6
Treacle, canned	75g portion	226	38.6	1.7	7.2
with jam, canned	100g	299	49.8	2.6	9.9
with jam, canned	75g portion	224	37.4	2.0	7.4
Trifle					
Fruit cocktail, individual	100g	182	23.1	2.5	2.6
Fruit cocktail, individual	113g carton	206	26.1	2.8	9.9
Home-made	100g	160	22.3	3.6	6.3
Home-made	170g portion	272	37.9	6.1	10.7
Home-made, with cream	100g	166	19.5	2.4	9.2
Home-made, with cream.	170g portion	282	31.2	4.1	15.6
Milk chocolate, individual	100g	282	25.1	4.7	18.2
Milk chocolate, individual	105g carton	296	26.4	4.9	19.1
Raspberry, individual	100g	173	21.1	2.5	8.7
Raspberry, individual	113g carton	195	23.8	2.8	9.8

Specific	Amount	Kcals	Carb	Prot	Fat
Yoghurt					
Greek, strained	100g	115	2.0	6.4	9.1
Greek, strained	150g serving	173	3.0	9.6	13.7
Low-fat, fruit	100g	90	17.9	4.1	0.7
Low-fat, fruit	150g pot	135	26.9	6.2	1.1
Low-fat, plain	100g	56	7.5	5.1	0.8
Low-fat, plain	150g pot	84	11.3	7.7	1.2
Very low- fat, fruit	100g	45	6.3	5.2	0.1
Very low- fat, fruit	150g pot	55	7.9	6.5	0.1
Whole milk, fruit	100g	105	15.7	5.1	2.8
Whole milk, fruit	150g pot	158	23.6	7.7	4.2
Whole milk, plain	100g	79	7.8	5.7	3.0
Whole milk, plain	150g pot	119	11.7	8.6	4.5

223

SOUPS, SAUCES AND MISCELLANEOUS

Specific	Amount	Kcals	Carb	Prot	Fat
Chutney					
Apple	100g	201	52.2	0.9	0.2
Apple	40g portion	80	20.9	0.4	0.1
Apple	1 heaped tsp [15g]	30	7.8	0.1	trace
Mango	100g	285	49.5	0.4	10.9
Mango	40 portion	114	19.8	0.2	4.4
Mango	1 heaped tsp [15g]	43	7.4	0.1	1.6
Tomato	100g	161	40.9	1.2	0.4
Tomato	40g portion	64	16.4	0.5	0.2
Tomato	1 heaped tsp [15g]	24	6.1	0.2	0.1
Miscellaneous					
Baking powder	100g	163	37.8	5.2	trace
Baking powder	1 level tsp	7	1.5	0.2	trace
Bovril	100g	169	2.9	38.0	0.7
Bovril	portion for bread [3g]	5	0.1	1.1	trace
Bovril	1 level tsp [9g]	15	0.3	3.4	trace
Gelatine	100g	338	0	84	0
Gravy granules, made with water	100g	462	40.6	4.4	32.5

SPECIFIC	AMOUNT	KCALS	CARB	PROT	FAT
Gravy granules, made					
with water	medium portion [70g]	323	28.4	3.1	22.8
Marmite	100g	172	1.8	39.7	0.7
Marmite	portion for bread [3g]	5	0.1	1.2	trace
Marmite	1 level tsp [9g]	15	0.2	3.6	0.1
Mustard, smooth	100g	139	9.7	7.1	8.2
Mustard smooth	1 level tsp [8g]	11	0.8	0.6	0.7
Mustard, wholegrain	100g	140	4.2	8.2	10.2
Mustard, wholegrain	1 level tsp	11	0.3	0.7	0.8
Oxo cubes	100g	229	12.0	38.3	3.4
Oxo cubes	1 cube [7g]	16	0.8	2.7	0.2
Salt	100g	0	0	0	0
Salt	1 tsp	0	0	0	0
Vinegar	100g	4	0.6	0.4	0
Vinegar	1 tbsp [15g]	1	0.1	0.1	0
Yeast, baker's compressed	100g	5	1.1	11.4	0.4
Yeast, dried	100g	169	3.5	35.6	1.5
Pickle					
Sweet	100g	134	34.4	0.6	0.3
Sweet	40g portion	54	13.8	0.2	0.1
Sweet	1 heaped tsp [15g]	20	5.2	trace	trace

SPECIFIC	AMOUNT	KCALS	CARB	PROT	FAT
Salad dressing					
French dressing	100g	649	0.1	0.3	72.1
French dressing	15g portion	97	trace	trace	10.8
Mayonnaise	100g	691	1.7	1.1	75.6
Mayonnaise	30g portion	207	0.5	0.3	22.7
Mayonnaise	1 tbsp [33g]	68	0.2	0.1	7.5
Salad cream	100g	348	16.7	1.5	31.0
Salad cream	30g portion	104	5.0	0.5	9.3
Salad cream, reduced calorie	100g	194	9.4	1.0	17.2
Salad cream, reduced calorie	30g portion	58	2.8	0.3	5.2
Sauce					
Barbecue	100g	75	12.2	1.8	1.8
Barbecue sauce	30g portion	23	3.7	0.5	0.5
Bread sauce, made with semi-skimmed milk	100g	93	12.8	4.3	3.1
Bread sauce, made with semi-skimmed milk	45g portion	42	5.8	1.9	1.4
Bread sauce, made with whole milk	100g	110	12.6	4.2	5.1
Bread sauce, made with whole milk	45g portion	50	5.7	9.2	11.2
Brown sauce, bottled	100g	99	25.2	1.1	0
Brown sauce, bottled	30g portion	29.7	7.6	0.3	0

227

Specific	Amount	Kcals	Carb	Prot	Fat
Cheese sauce, made with semi-skimmed milk	100g	179	9.1	8.1	12.6
Cheese sauce, made with semi-skimmed milk	medium portion [60g]	107	5.5	4.9	7.6
Cheese sauce, made with whole milk	100g	197	8.0	14.6	8.7
Cheese sauce, made with whole milk	medium portion [60g]	118	5.4	4.8	8.7
Cheese sauce, packet mix, made with semi-skimmed milk	100g	90	9.5	5.4	3.8
Cheese sauce, packet mix, made with semi-skimmed milk	medium portion [60g]	54	5.7	3.2	2.3
Cheese sauce, packet mix, made with whole milk	100g	110	9.3	5.3	6.1
Cheese sauce, packet mix, made with whole milk	medium portion [60g]	66	5.6	3.2	3.7
Cook-in sauces, canned, average	100g	43	8.3	1.1	0.8
Cook-in sauces, canned, average	115g portion	49	9.5	1.3	0.9
Curry sauce, canned	100g	78	7.1	1.5	5.0
Curry sauce, canned	115g portion	90	8.2	1.7	5.8
Horseradish sauce	100g	153	17.9	2.5	8.4
Horseradish sauce	15g portion	23	2.7	0.4	1.3
Mint sauce	100g	87	21.5	1.6	trace
Mint sauce	10g portion	8.7	2.2	0.2	trace
Onion sauce, made with semi-skimmed milk	100g	86	8.4	2.9	5.0

228

SPECIFIC	AMOUNT	KCALS	CARB	PROT	FAT
Onion sauce, made with semi-skimmed milk	medium portion [60g]	52	5.0	1.7	3.0
Onion sauce, made with whole milk	100g	99	8.3	2.8	6.5
Onion sauce, made with whole milk	medium portion [60g]	60	5.0	1.7	3.9
Pasta sauce, tomato based	100g	47	6.9	2.0	1.5
Pasta sauce, tomato based	90g portion	42	6.2	1.8	1.4
Soy sauce	100g	64	8.3	8.7	0
Soy sauce	1 tsp [5g]	3	0.4	0.4	0
Tomato ketchup	100g	98	24.0	2.1	trace
Tomato ketchup	30g portion	29	7.2	0.6	trace
Tomato sauce, home-made	100g	89	8.6	2.2	5.5
Tomato sauce, home-made	90g portion	80	7.7	2.0	5.0
White sauce, savoury, made with semi-skimmed milk	100g	128	11.1	4.2	7.8
White sauce, savoury, made with semi-skimmed milk	medium portion [60g]	77	6.6	2.5	4.7
White sauce, savoury, made with whole milk	100g	150	10.9	4.1	10.3
White sauce, savoury, made with whole milk	medium portion [60g]	90	6.5	2.5	6.2
White sauce, sweet, made with semi-skimmed milk	100g	150	18.8	3.9	7.2
White sauce, sweet, made with semi-skimmed milk	medium portion [60g]	90	11.3	2.3	4.3

Specific	Amount	Kcals	Carb	Prot	Fat
White sauce, sweet, made with whole milk	100g	170	18.6	3.8	9.5
White sauce, sweet, made with whole milk	medium portion [60g]	102	11.2	2.3	5.7
Soup					
Chicken noodle, dried, ready to serve	100g	20	3.7	0.8	0.3
Chicken noodle, dried, ready to serve	medium portion [220g]	44	8.1	1.8	0.7
Cream of chicken, canned, ready to serve	100g	58	4.5	1.7	3.8
Cream of chicken, canned, ready to serve	medium portion [220g]	128	9.9	3.7	8.4
Cream of chicken, condensed, canned	100g	98	6.0	2.6	7.2
Cream of chicken, condensed, diluted, ready to serve	100g	49	3.0	1.3	3.6
Cream of chicken, condensed, diluted, ready to serve	medium portion [220g]	108	6.6	2.9	7.9
Cream of mushroom soup, canned, ready to serve	100g	53	3.9	1.1	3.8
Cream of mushroom, canned, ready to serve	medium portion [220g]	117	8.6	2.4	8.4
Cream of tomato, canned, ready to serve	100g	55	5.9	0.8	3.3
Cream of tomato, canned, ready to serve	medium portion [220g]	121	13.0	1.8	7.3

SPECIFIC	AMOUNT	KCALS	CARB	PROT	FAT
Cream of tomato, condensed, canned	100g	123	14.6	1.7	6.8
Cream of tomato, condensed, diluted, ready to serve	100g	62	7.3	0.9	3.4
Cream of tomato, condensed, diluted, ready to serve	medium portion [220g]	136	16.1	2.0	7.5
Instant soup powder, average, made with water, ready to serve	100g	64	10.5	1.1	2.3
Instant soup powder, average, made with water, ready to serve	medium portion [220g]	141	23	2.4	5.1
Lentil, home-made	100g	99	12.7	4.4	3.8
Lentil, home-made	medium portion [220g]	218	27.9	9.7	8.4
Low-calorie, average, canned	100g	20	4.0	0.9	0.2
Low-calorie, average, canned	medium portion [220g]	44	8.8	2.0	0.4
Minestrone, dried, ready to serve	100g	298	47.6	10.1	8.8
Minestrone, dried, ready to serve	medium portion [220g]	656	104.7	22.2	19.4
Oxtail, canned, ready to serve	100g	44	5.1	2.4	1.7
Oxtail, canned, ready to serve	medium portion [220g]	97	11.2	5.3	3.7
Oxtail, dried, ready to serve	100g	27	3.9	1.4	0.8
Oxtail, dried, ready to serve	medium portion [220g]	59	8.6	3.1	1.8
Tomato, dried, ready to serve	100g	31	6.3	0.6	0.5
Tomato, dried, ready to serve	medium portion [220g]	68	13.9	1.3	1.1
Vegetable, canned, ready to serve	100g	37	6.7	1.5	0.7
Vegetable, canned, ready to serve	medium portion [220g]	81	14.7	3.3	1.5

SUGAR, SYRUPS AND PRESERVES

SPECIFIC	AMOUNT	KCALS	CARB	PROT	FAT
Preserves					
Jam, fruit	100g	261	69.0	0.6	0
Jam, fruit	15g portion for bread	39	10.4	0.1	0
Jam, fruit	1 heaped tsp [18g]	47	12.4	0.1	0
Jam, stone fruit	100g	261	69.3	0.4	0
Jam, stone fruit	15g portion for bread	39	10.4	0.1	0
Jam, stone fruit	1 heaped tsp [18g]	47	12.5	0.1	0
Jam, reduced sugar	100g	123	31.9	0.5	0
Jam, reduced sugar	15g portion for bread	18	4.8	0.1	0
Jam, reduced sugar	1 heaped tsp [18g]	22	5.7	0.1	0
Lemon curd	100g	283	62.7	0.6	5.1
Lemon curd	15g portion for bread	42	9.4	0.1	0.8
Lemon curd	1 heaped tsp [18g]	51	11.3	0.1	0.9
Marmalade	100g	261	69.5	0.1	0
Marmalade	15g portion for bread	39	10.4	trace	0
Marmalade	1 heaped tsp [18g]	47	12.5	trace	0
Mincemeat	100g	274	62.1	0.6	4.3
Spread					
Chocolate nut	100g	549	60.5	6.2	33.0

Specific	Amount	Kcals	Carb	Prot	Fat
Chocolate nut	20g portion for bread	110	12.1	1.2	6.6
Chocolate nut	1 heaped tsp [16g]	88	9.7	1.0	5.3
Honey	100g	288	76.4	0.4	0
Honey	20g portion for bread	58	15.3	0.1	0
Honey	1 heaped tsp [17g]	49	13.0	0.1	0
Honey & comb	100g	281	74.4	0.6	4.6
Honey & comb	20g portion for bread	56	14.9	0.1	0.9
Sugar					
Demerara	100g	394	104.5	0.5	0
Demerara	1 tsp [20g]	79	20.9	0.1	0
Demerara	1 level tsp [4g]	16	4.2	trace	0
Demerara	7g individual sachet	28	7.3	trace	0
Glucose liquid	100g	318	84.7	trace	0
White	100g	394	105.0	trace	0
White	1 tbsp [20g]	79	21.0	trace	0
White	1 level tsp [4g]	16	4.2	trace	0
White	1 cube [5g]	20	5.3	trace	0
Treacle					
Black	100g	257	67.2	1.2	0

Specific	Amount	Kcals	Carb	Prot	Fat
Syrup Golden	100g	298	79.0	0.3	0

FATS AND OILS

SPECIFIC	AMOUNT	KCALS	CARB	PROT	FAT
Animal fat					
Compound cooking fat	100g	894	trace	trace	99.3
Dripping, beef	100g	891	trace	trace	99.0
Lard	100g	891	trace	trace	99.0
Suet, shredded	100g	826	12.1	trace	86.7
Ghee					
Butter	100g	898	trace	trace	99.8
Palm	100g	897	trace	trace	99.7
Vegetable	100g	898	trace	trace	99.8
Oil					
Coconut oil	100g	899	0	trace	99.9
Cod liver oil	100g	899	0	trace	99.9
Corn oil	100g	899	0	trace	99.9
Cottonseed oil	100g	899	0	trace	99.9
Olive oil	100g	899	0	trace	99.9
Palm oil	100g	899	0	trace	99.9
Peanut oil	100g	899	0	trace	99.9
Rapeseed oil	100g	899	0	trace	99.9

SPECIFIC	AMOUNT	KCALS	CARB	PROT	FAT
Safflower oil	100g	899	0	trace	99.9
Sesame oil	100g	881	0	0.2	99.7
Soya oil	100g	899	0	trace	99.9
Sunflower seed oil	100g	899	0	trace	99.9
Vegetable oil, blended, average	100g	899	0	trace	99.9
Wheatgerm oil	100g	899	0	trace	99.9
Spreading fat					
Butter	100g	737	trace	0.5	81.7
Dairy/fat spread	100g	662	trace	0.4	73.4
Low fat spread	100g	390	0.5	5.8	40.5
Margarine, hard, animal and vegetable fat	100g	739	1.0	0.2	81.6
Margarine, hard, vegetable fat only	100g	739	1.0	0.2	81.6
Margarine, soft, animal and vegetable fat	100g	739	1.0	0.2	81.6
Margarine, soft, vegetable fat only	100g	739	1.0	0.2	81.6
Margarine, polyunsaturated	100g	739	1.0	0.2	81.6
Very low fat spread	100g	273	3.6	8.3	25.0

ALCOHOLIC BEVERAGES

Specific	Amount	Kcals	Carb	Prot	Fat
Ale					
Bottled, brown	100ml	28	3	trace	nil
Bottled, brown	1 pt	159	17	trace	nil
Bottled, pale	100ml	32	2	trace	nil
Bottled, pale	1 pt	182	11.4	trace	nil
Strong	100ml	72	6.1	trace	nil
Strong	1 pt	409	34.6	trace	nil
Beer					
Bitter, canned	100ml	32	2.3	trace	nil
Bitter, canned	1 pt	182	13.1	trace	nil
Bitter, draught	100ml	32	2.3	trace	nil
Bitter, draught	1 pt	182	13.1	trace	nil
Bitter, keg	100ml	31	2.3	trace	nil
Bitter, keg	1 pt	1769	13.1	trace	nil
Mild, draught	100ml	25	1.6	trace	nil
Mild, draught	1 pt	142	9.1	trace	nil
Stout	100ml	37	4.2	trace	nil
Stout	1 pt	210	23.5	trace	nil
Stout, extra	100ml	39	2.1	trace	nil

Specific	Amount	Kcals	Carb	Prot	Fat
Stout, extra	1 pt	222	11.9	trace	nil
Cider					
Dry	100ml	36	2.6	trace	nil
Dry	1 pt	204	14.8	trace	nil
Sweet	100ml	42	4.3	trace	nil
Sweet	1 pt	238	24.4	trace	nil
Vintage	100ml	101	7.3	trace	nil
Vintage	1 pt	573	41.5	trace	nil
Fortified Wine					
Port	30ml	47	3.6	trace	nil
Sherry, dry	30ml	35	0.5	trace	nil
Sherry, medium	30ml	35	1.0	trace	nil
Sherry, sweet	30ml	43	2	trace	nil
Lager					
Bottled	100ml	29	1.5	trace	nil
Bottled	1 pt	165	8.5	trace	nil
Spirits					
Brandy, 40% proof	30ml	65	trace	trace	nil
Gin, 40% proof	30ml	65	trace	trace	nil

SPECIFIC	AMOUNT	KCALS	CARB	PROT	FAT
Rum, 40% proof	30ml	65	trace	trace	nil
Vodka, 40% proof	30ml	65	trace	trace	nil
Whisky, 40% proof	30ml	65	trace	trace	nil
Wine					
Red	100ml	68	0.3	trace	nil
Red	1 bottle [750ml]	510	2.3	trace	nil
Red	1 glass [120ml]	82	0.4	trace	nil
Rose, medium	100ml	71	2.5	trace	nil
Rose, medium	1bottle [750ml]	533	18.8	trace	nil
Rose, medium	1 glass [120ml]	853	3.0	trace	nil
White, dry	100ml	66	0.6	trace	nil
White, dry	1 bottle [750ml]	495	4.5	trace	nil
White, dry	1 glass [120ml]	79	0.7	trace	nil
White, medium	100ml	75	3.4	trace	nil
White, medium	1 bottle [750ml]	563	25.5	trace	nil
White, medium	1 glass [120ml]	90	4.1	trace	nil
White, sparkling	100ml	76	1.4	trace	nil
White, sparkling	1 bottle [750ml]	570	10.5	trace	nil
White, sparkling	1 glass [120ml]	91	1.7	trace	nil
White, sweet	100ml	94	5.9	trace	nil
White, sweet	1 bottle [750ml]	705	44.3	trace	nil
White, sweet	1 glass [120ml]	113	53.2	trace	nil

NON-ALCOHOLIC BEVERAGES

SPECIFIC	AMOUNT	KCALS	CARB	PROT	FAT
Bournvita					
Semi-skimmed milk	100g	58	7.8	3.5	1.6
Semi-skimmed milk	1 mug [260g]	151	20.3	9.1	4.2
Whole milk	100g	76	7.6	3.4	3.8
Whole milk	1 mug [260g]	198	19.8	8.9	9.9
Powder	100g	341	79.0	7.7	1.5
Powder	portion [8g]	27	6.3	0.6	0.1
Build-up					
Semi-skimmed milk	100g	80	11.9	5.7	1.5
Semi-skimmed milk	1 mug [260g]	208	30.9	14.8	3.9
Whole milk	100g	98	11.7	5.6	3.6
Whole milk	1 mug [260g]	255	30.4	14.6	9.4
Carbonated drink					
Coca-cola	100g	36	10.5	trace	0
Coca-cola	can [330g]	119	5.0	trace	0
Lemonade, bottled	100g	21	5.6	trace	0
Lemonade, bottled	1 glass [200g]	42	11.2	trace	0

SPECIFIC	AMOUNT	KCALS	CARB	PROT	FAT
Lucozade, bottled	100g	67	18.0	trace	0
Lucozade, bottled	1 glass [200g]	134	36.0	trace	0
Cocoa					
Semi-skimmed milk	100g	57	7.0	3.5	1.9
Semi-skimmed milk	1 mug [260g]	148	18.2	22.9	4.9
Whole milk	100g	76	6.8	3.4	4.2
Whole milk	1 mug [260g]	198	17.7	8.8	10.9
Powder	100g	312	11.5	18.5	21.7
Powder	1 tsp [6g]	19	0.7	1.1	1.3
Coffee					
Instant, powder	100g	11.0	14.6	0	
Instant, powder	1 tsp [2g]	9	0.2	0.3	0
Instant, 30g of whole milk	1 mug	22	1.6	1.3	1.2
Instant, without milk or sugar	1 mug [260g]	2	0.2	0.3	0
Coffeemate					
Powder	100g	540	57.3	2.7	34.9
Powder	portion [6g]	32	3.4	0.2	2.1
Complan					
Sweet, water	100g	96	13.4	4.5	3.1

244

SPECIFIC	AMOUNT	KCALS	CARB	PROT	FAT
Sweet, water	1 mug [260g]	250	34.8	11.7	8.1
Sweet, whole milk	100g	145	16.9	6.9	6.1
Sweet, whole milk	1 mug [260g]	377	43.9	17.9	15.9
Sweet, powder	100g	430	57.9	20.0	14.0
Cordial					
Lime juice cordial, undiluted	100g	112	29.8	0.1	0
Lime juice cordial, undiluted	1 glass [40g]	45	11.9	trace	0
Rosehip syrup, undiluted	100g	232	4.8	trace	0
Rosehip syrup, undiluted	1 glass [40g]	93	1.9	trace	0
Drinking chocolate					
Semi-skimmed milk	100g	71	10.8	3.5	1.9
Semi-skimmed milk	1 mug [260g]	185	28.1	9.1	4.9
Whole milk	100g	90	10.6	3.4	4.1
Whole milk	1 mug [260g]	234	27.6	8.8	10.7
Powder	100g	366	77.4	5.5	6.0
Powder	1 mug [18g]	66	13.9	1.0	1.1
Horlicks					
Instant, water	100g	51	10.1	2.4	0.5
Instant, water	1 mug [260g]	133	26.6	6.2	1.3
Semi-skimmed milk	100g	81	12.9	4.3	1.9

SPECIFIC	AMOUNT	KCALS	CARB	PROT	FAT
Semi-skimmed milk	1 mug [260g]	211	33.5	11.2	4.9
Whole milk	100g	99	12.7	4.2	3.9
Whole milk	1 mug [260g]	257	33.0	10.9	10.1
Powder	100g	378	78.0	12.4	4.0
Powder	portion [25g]	945	19.5	0.4	1.0
Powder, low fat, instant	portion [32g]	119	23.3	5.6	1.1
Powder, low fat, instant	100g	373	72.9	17.4	3.3
Juice					
Apple juice, unsweetened	100g	38	9.9	0.1	0.1
Apple juice, unsweetened	1 glass [200g]	76	328	0.2	0.2
Grape juice, unsweetened	100g	46	11.7	0.3	0.1
Grape juice, unsweetened	1 glass [200g]	92	23.4	0.6	0.2
Grapefruit juice, unsweetened	100g	33	8.3	0.4	0.1
Grapefruit juice, unsweetened	1 glass [200g]	66	16.6	0.8	0.2
Lemon juice, unsweetened	100g	7	1.6	0.3	trace
Lemon juice, unsweetened	1 tbsp [15g]	1	0.2	trace	trace
Orange juice, unsweetened	100g	36	8.8	0.5	0.1
Orange juice, unsweetened	1 glass [200g]	72	17.6	1.0	0.2
Pineapple juice, unsweetened	100g	41	10.5	0.3	0.1
Pineapple juice, unsweetened	1 glass [200g]	82	21.0	0.6	0.2
Tomato juice	100g	14	3.0	0.8	trace
Tomato juice	1 glass [200g]	28	6.0	1.6	trace

SPECIFIC	AMOUNT	KCALS	CARB	PROT	FAT
Milk shake					
Semi-skimmed milk	1 glass [200g]	138	22.6	6.4	3.2
Semi-skimmed milk	100g	69	11.3	3.2	1.6
Whole milk	100g	87	11.1	3.1	3.7
Whole milk	1 glass [200g]	174	22.2	6.2	7.4
Powder	100g	388	98.3	1.3	1.6
Powder	portion [15g]	58	14.7	0.2	0.2
Thick, take-away	100g	90	13.2	2.9	3.2
Thick, take-away	ave. portion [300g]	270	39.6	8.7	9.6
Ovaltine					
Semi-skimmed milk	100g	79	13.0	3.9	1.7
Semi-skimmed milk	1 mug [260g]	205	33.8	10.1	4.4
Whole milk	100g	97	12.9	3.8	3.8
Whole milk	1 mug [260g]	252	4.9	9.9	9.9
Powder	100g	358	79.4	9.0	2.7
Powder	portion [25g]	90	19.9	2.3	0.7
Squash					
Orange drink, undiluted	100g	107	28.5	trace	0
Orange drink, undiluted	1 glass [40g]	43	11.4	trace	0
Ribena	100g	228	60.8	0.1	0
Ribena	1 glass [40g]	91	24.3	trace	0

SPECIFIC	AMOUNT	KCALS	CARB	PROT	FAT
Tea					
No milk or sugar	100g	trace	trace	0.1	trace
No milk or sugar	1 cup [200g]	trace	trace	0.2	trace
With 30g of whole milk	1 cup [200g]	20	1.4	1.2	1.2

Index to Calories